ADVAN
The Art c,

MW01040399

"John Moses displays his own artistry and skill in this account of how Thomas Merton explores the mystery of God. It exhibits Merton's life, with fresh and compelling insight, as a canvas on which the rich and raw intensity of human experience is displayed. This is a book with which to spend time in reflection, prayer and delight. The sort of materials that Merton uses in his exploration are silence, desire, inter-relatedness, catholic Christendom, and intelligence in all its forms. Merton's words and images, half a century later, still touch the issues that define our life and our future, making this a compelling compendium of Christian wisdom."

—MARTIN WARNER, Bishop of Chichester

"John Moses breaks new ground in this scholarly yet accessible anthology based on Merton's curious 'blobs of ink'. He opens doors for us to get immersed in this complex monk's understanding of the cosmic dance of life, lived out in each of us in response to God's call. His interpretation of Merton's art is offered to be prayed, not merely read, for through his understanding of the nature and practice of prayer, Merton demonstrated a way of being alive that focuses the Christian hope for all whose awareness is awakened."

—REVEREND CANON DR. VINCENT STRUDWICK,
Honorary Fellow Kellogg College, University of Oxford,
author, *The Naked God: Wrestling for a Grace-ful Humanity.*

"This anthology of Thomas Merton's words and calligraphies is an inviting gateway into an experience of enrichment and deep wisdom. Thanks to John Moses, we can enjoyably explore this life-awakening selection."

—FIONA GARDNER, author, *The Only Mind Worth Having, Thomas Merton and the Child Mind,* and *Precious Thoughts*

"John Moses' anthology provides an accessible way to introduce the inspirational teaching of Thomas Merton to a new readership. Whether on a coffee table or in a chapel, the synthesis of art and reflective writing around central gospel themes reveal vividly how Merton's wisdom continues to speak across many diverse cultures today, both inside and outside the Church. Artist and wordsmith combine with beautiful simplicity, inviting us to engage with the profound questions around what it means to respond daily to the gospel of Jesus Christ in an ever changing and uncertain world."

—RIGHT REVEREND PAUL WILLIAMS, Bishop of Southwell & Nottingham

the art of
Thomas Merton

A DIVINE PASSION
IN WORD AND VISION

EDITED AND COMPILED BY

John Moses

franciscan
media
Cincinnati, Ohio

published by Crossroad Publishing Company (used by permission of the Merton Legacy Trust).

New Directions: *The Collected Poems of Thomas Merton*, copyright © 1944, 1949, 1963, by Our Lady of Gethsemani Monastery; copyright © 1946, 1948, by New Directions Publishing Corporation; copyright © 1977 by the Trustees of the Merton Legacy Trust; *New Seeds of Contemplation*, copyright © 1961 by The Abbey of Gethsemani.

Penguin Random House: Excerpts from *Conjectures of a Guilty Bystander*, copyright © 1965, 1966, by The Abbey of Gethsemani; used by permission of Doubleday, an imprint of the Knopf Doubleday Publishing Group, a division of Penguin Random House LLC; all rights reserved.

Photographs of the drawings of Thomas Merton are used by permission of the Merton Legacy Trust and the Thomas Merton Center at Bellarmine University.

Scripture passages have been taken from *New Revised Standard Version Bible,* copyright ©1989 by the Division of Christian Education of the National Council of the Churches of Christ in the U.S.A., and used by permission. All rights reserved.

Cover and book design by Mark Sullivan

LIBRARY OF CONGRESS CATALOGING-IN-PUBLICATION DATA
Names: Moses, John, editor.
Title: The art of Thomas Merton : a divine passion in word and vision / compiled and edited by John Moses ; foreword by Paul M. Pearson.
Description: Cincinnati : Franciscan Media, 2018. | Includes bibliographical references.
Identifiers: LCCN 2017052669 | ISBN 9781632531841 (trade paper)
Subjects: LCSH: Merton, Thomas, 1915-1968. | Merton, Thomas, 1915-1968—Quotations. | Christian art and symbolism.
Classification: LCC BX4705.M542 A78 2018 | DDC 271/.12502--dc23
LC record available at https://lccn.loc.gov/2017052669

ISBN 978-1-63253-184-1

Copyright ©2017, John Moses. All rights reserved.

Published by Franciscan Media
28 W. Liberty St.
Cincinnati, OH 45202
www.FranciscanMedia.org

Printed in the United States of America.
Printed on acid-free paper.
17 18 19 20 21   5 4 3 2 1

For
E and F
G and T and O
W and S

• • •

Either you look at the universe as a very poor creation out of which no one can make anything, or you look at your own life and your own part in the universe as infinitely rich, full of inexhaustible interest, opening out into infinite further possibilities for study and contemplation and interest and praise. Beyond all and in all is God.

• • •

Thomas Merton
A Search for Solitude

~CONTENTS~

~ACKNOWLEDGEMENTS~

I am extremely grateful to Dr. Paul M. Pearson, the Director of the Thomas Merton Center at Bellarmine University, for the Foreword he has generously provided and for the unfailing support he has given over recent years as I have pursued my study of Thomas Merton.

I am glad to acknowledge the permission that has been granted to use excerpts from Merton's writings in this anthology. Every attempt has been made to secure permission to use copyrighted material, and all such material is fully documented in the Notes at the back of this book. Readers will understand that Merton was writing before a time when inclusive language had become commonplace, and I hope it will be recognized that it has been necessary to keep faith with the actual words used by Merton.

I am grateful to the Merton Legacy Trust and the Merton Center for the permission that has been given for the use of the drawings in this anthology.

Members of staff at Franciscan Media have given great encouragement as the book has taken shape; Anne McCormick, one of the Merton Legacy Trustees, has been a tremendous help in the search for copyright permissions; and Jasmine Oakes has provided invaluable assistance in the preparation of the manuscript. I am most grateful.

—J.M.

~FOREWORD~

by Dr. Paul M. Pearson,
Director of the Thomas Merton Center

Thomas Merton's longtime friend and editor, Robert Giroux, recounted on a number of occasions the letters he sometimes received from readers upset by Merton's views, writing to Giroux asking him to "Tell this talking Trappist who took a vow of silence to *shut up!*"[1] Certainly from within the cloister of a religious order, one with a reputation for its strong tradition of silence and which, up until the time of the Second Vatican Council, made use of sign language in lieu of speaking, Thomas Merton's literary eloquence literally flooded the market over the course of his relatively short writing career, just twenty years from the publication of his autobiography in October 1948 until his accidental death in December 1968. Merton's prominence on the *New York Times* best-seller list in the late forties led Charles Poore, in a story published on December 31, 1949, to have one of his characters quip that "the ten outstanding books of the nineteen fifties...will mostly be written by Thomas Merton."[2]

Merton's eloquence, this outpouring of so many words, flowed from his restless, indeed relentless, searching and striving for the one true *Word*, for the *Divine Logos*. Over the years not a few of his readers have been distracted by various aspects of his life and writings—most notably, in his own lifetime, as he moved from the world-denying monk of his early monastic years to the world-embracing monk of the final decade of his life. As Merton came to the realization that he was in the monastery for the world and that his monastic vocation and spiritual journey demanded that he address many of the major issues of his day, many of those who had devoured his spiritual writings found his social writings impossible to stomach. Many early devotees stopped reading him, church authorities silenced him from publishing on these issues, and some former readers even took to publicly burning his books as he noted in a letter to Czeslaw Milosz: "Conservative Catholics in Louisville are burning my books because I'm opposed to the Viet Nam War."[3]

Subsequently in the years after his death, readers have been turned off by other aspects of his writing, such as the revelation of his affair with a nurse in 1966, or by misunderstandings of his dialogue with peoples of other faiths. Merton's interfaith dialogue was no wishy-washy new age synthesis, he didn't go to Asia in the fall of 1968 to leave the Catholic Church and to become a Buddhist as some conservative Catholics would suggest. No, Merton was so deeply rooted in his own Catholic Christian tradition that he was able to truly dialogue—as the Dalai Lama would write in his autobiography *Freedom in Exile* "It was Thomas Merton who introduced me to the real meaning of the word Christian."[4]

Thomas Merton's abbot at the time of his death, Flavian Burns, certainly understood the complexity of this man and warned Merton's official biographer John Howard Griffin that he was "dealing with the life of an authentic saint who utterly refused to cooperate in edifying anyone. You are dealing with a man of such complexity, such guts, such secrecy, that you will be overwhelmed. What few people know is that every morning he spent three hours in uninterrupted mental prayer and that in the end he was approaching the highest solution," adding that he was "the most absolute monk.... All of his difficulties sprang from the search to become more and more absolute as a monk (not the contrary, as so many people think). He was stripping away everything in his move toward total solitude with God."[5]

It is this Merton, the one spoken of by Flavian Burns, that you the reader will discover in the feast that John Moses has prepared for you in these pages. In passages selected from the broadest selection of Merton's writings, it is the "absolute monk" who will be encountered, the monk whose words and images welled up and overflowed from his hours of silent prayer to quench the thirst of seekers everywhere. Knowing the source of Merton's inspiration requires of the reader, as Moses himself suggests, praying this anthology.

The power of the image was as equally important to Merton as the word. As the son of artists, artistic expression was integral to Merton, and the images selected by Moses for this volume are another gateway for you the reader to enter into prayer and wonderment. Merton wrote to one correspondent that his calligraphies are "pure and simple as they are, and they should lay no claim to being anything but themselves" and that "each time one sees them is the first time."[6] These calligraphies can serve as an invitation to us to break through the torrent of images that we are constantly bombarded with to that inner radiance of being, that consciousness of paradise within each and every one of us, to that image of God in which we were created—an invitation to discover what Merton calls the "cosmic dance which...beats in our very blood."[7]

This is not a book to speed-read, to read for study or for the acquisition of knowledge. No, it demands for the words to be read, and the images gazed upon, in the manner of the practice of *Lectio Divina*, allowing God to speak to you by reading and looking attentively, peacefully, and reflectively until a word, phrase, or image strikes the imagination or the heart. And, when this happens, then prayerfully pausing, allowing, in the words of the poet Rainer Maria Rilke, for "its meaning" to "spread through the blood," to spread to our heart, and to allow our experience of God's love and mercy to overflow out to the world.

~PREFACE~

The genius of Thomas Merton is to be found in his passion for God. It dominated the story of his life and enabled him to speak to people all over the world. His several vocations, which inform our perception of the man, must not be allowed, however, to obscure the fact that he brought to his life and work the instincts and the characteristics of a true artist. Merton knew what it meant to enter the depths of our experience, to penetrate the bland certainties with which we console ourselves, to hold up a mirror to the face and to the pain of our world, to be in touch with life's deepest rhythms. In his writings and in his drawings, he spoke of the Divine Passion that alone can give some sense of identity and purpose. In common with every great artist, he made it possible to set our immediate concerns within the context of the universal human drama.

Thomas Merton continues to speak with a voice that is insightful, compelling, and prophetic. His extensive writings provide ample scope for any compiler who attempts to set before the reader a coherent introduction to his thought, his questions, his concerns, his passions. Words mattered: they were Merton's stock-in-trade, his first and most characteristic art form. Few people have been the subject of so much scrutiny and interpretation, but an anthology enables Merton to speak for himself, and it allows the reader to engage directly with a man who—fifty years after his death—remains a surprisingly contemporary figure, addressing time and again the issues that matter to us and to our world.

Those who are unfamiliar with Merton's story will be surprised to discover that a man who had so much to say about so many things was a Trappist monk, committed to a life of withdrawal from the world, of silence and solitude. It is not the least of the many contradictions that Merton presents that *for him* the religious vocation, the religious life, should have been the seedbed in which he found his vocations as a religious, a writer, a contemplative, a social critic, and an ecumenist. He spoke of himself as a man whose "life is almost totally paradoxical,"[1] and yet—as he himself acknowledged—it was the contradictions, together with the "moments of depression and despair,"[2] that proved to be so instructive, so formative. For Merton, they were "signs of God's mercy";[3] for us, they might be seen with the advantage of hindsight as the framework within which he found his prophetic awareness and his prophetic voice.

What can be seen as we follow the twists and turns of Merton's parallel vocations is a passion for God, for the truth about himself, and for the world in which he lived. Abbot Timothy Kelly, who had served in the novitiate under Merton in the late 1950s, spoke of him as someone who was "always very positive, always very present to life, and very present to the moment."[4] Merton's mind was ever alert; and yet in solitude, and above all in contemplative prayer, he sought depths which his inquiring mind could never fully encompass or possess. It was as though in exploring the depths within himself he was entering the depths with others, finding our mutual at-one-ness in God. The description of Merton as "a man who opened doors"[5] is confirmed year by year in the experience of people all over the world who find in Merton something of their own story: the questions to which there is no easy answer, the contradictions of discipleship, the discontents, but also the ideal to which we aspire—the search for God.

It is this recognition of Thomas Merton as a man who makes things possible for other people that has influenced the shape and the content of this anthology so that it might serve not only as an introduction to his thought but also as an aid to private devotion, a signpost for our personal journeys of discernment and encounter. *The Art of Thomas Merton* brings together entries from Merton's journals, extracts from his letters, quotations from his books and his countless articles, and lines from his poetry. The quotations have been brought together in six sections—"Encountering God," "Living the Gospel," "Learning to Pray," "Embracing the World," "The Church Looking Beyond Itself," and "On Being in Christ"—and within each section quotations are clustered around several related themes.

Some compilers might well have chosen other quotations—there is certainly no lack of choice—but I have selected those that speak most directly of the things that mattered to Merton so that he might continue to speak to us. It follows necessarily that it is not sufficient for the reader merely to be a passive recipient of another man's thoughts. The quotations ask that we might find their meaning *for us*. It occurs to me, therefore, that some might be assisted in this journey of exploration if each theme can be prefaced by one of Merton's drawings taking its place alongside the words, and serving as a resting place along the way for those who use this anthology.

Merton's drawings have received little attention over the years from those who have attempted to understand his story and his meaning, but Dr. Roger Lipsey's book *Angelic Mistakes*[6] has done much to rectify this omission and to introduce us to the visual art that mattered so much to Merton. His drawings—like his photographs—were exercises in quiet reflection. His photography captures the innate beauty of the ordinary, and his abstract drawings convey something of the awareness through silence that he was always eager to explore.

Merton's art encompassed over the years a wide variety of styles and techniques. Simple line drawings gave place to brush and ink drawings, and these in turn gave place to the creation of images through a unique printmaking technique.[7] His poetry was described by one reviewer as "maddeningly disparate...zany... confronting and challenging our conventional images,"[8] and a similar judgement might well be made where his drawings, and especially his calligraphies, are concerned. He was pleased with what he achieved, but he was aware of his limitations as a visual artist and refused to take his drawings too seriously. Perhaps only Merton with a wry self-mocking humor could speak of his work as "strange blobs of ink."[9] There is certainly much that might be considered inconsequential, but it is possible to see in his drawings something of the mental energy, the openness to new possibilities and the freedom of interpretation that characterized so many of his activities.

What Merton referred to as his "brush and ink drawings"[10] or his "abstract calligraphies"[11] owed much to the influence of Zen Buddhism and were especially important in the last decade of his life. They were exercises in observation and engagement. He rarely offers an interpretation, and in refusing to provide a title for so much of his visual art, he is setting the observer free to find his or her own meaning.

For Merton, calligraphies were "signs and ciphers of energy."[12] They were not to be pigeonholed in some conventional hierarchy of artistic forms. "Momentary and unique, free, undetermined and inconclusive"—these were the words that Merton used to indicate what he was feeling after.[13] "Each stroke is so to speak first and last, all goes in one breath, one brushful of ink, and the result is a statement of itself that is 'right' insofar as it says nothing 'about' anything else under the sun."[14]

Merton was seeking new visual experiences—what he called

"summonses to awareness"[15]—set free from the predictable categories of "religious" art. He wanted to press forward, to explore, to make new connections. They can therefore be properly understood only in the light of that discovery of God—and that parallel journey of self-discovery—in which he was continually caught up. And it is precisely here that the drawings might have a part to play as they invite us to stop, and reflect, and surprise ourselves by new depths of awareness and understanding.

Merton's hope that his drawings might "continue to awaken possibilities"[16] provides the best possible introduction to any use that might be made of the drawings and the words that constitute this anthology. It must be acknowledged, however, that the assignment of particular drawings to specific themes in this anthology, together with a brief reflection in every case, is entirely my responsibility. Some might find that the drawings do not necessarily speak to them; some will not necessarily make the connections I have made between drawings and themes and words. All that matters is that those who use this anthology might find in words and drawings something of the Divine Passion—God's search for us and our search for God—that lay at the heart of Merton's journey and of all that he had to say.

It is important to suggest that those who want to explore Merton through their reading—or should that be through their praying?—of this anthology should proceed slowly. Do not be in a hurry. Do not take more than one theme at a time. Do not hesitate to stay with one quotation, reading it aloud if that is helpful, exploring it, finding its meaning *for you*. There are, however, two questions that all who use this anthology might address. First, does it enable us to respond more fully to the Gospel invitation to enter into life? Secondly, does it point us outwards, enabling us to find something of that passion for the world that was inseparable in Merton's experience from his passion for God? Merton was a sublime wordsmith, but he also knew the limitations of words. What matters is that words lead into thought, that thought leads into prayer, that prayer leads into love. Thomas Merton would have asked for nothing more.

—JOHN MOSES

~THOMAS MERTON: A PROFILE~

Thomas Merton was born on January 31, 1915. His parents, who had met as art students in Paris, had settled after their marriage at Prades, a small French town near the Spanish border.

Merton's childhood and adolescence were punctuated by a series of tragedies: the death of his mother (1921); the unsettled years as he traveled with or without his father and his younger brother to the United States, to Bermuda, to France, to England (1921–29); the death of his father (1931); the rejection by his godfather and guardian after a disastrous year at Cambridge (1934).

His student years at Columbia University (1935–39) saw his early endeavors to write and be published, the importance of friendships, a preoccupation with questions of social justice, his reception into the Roman Catholic Church, the first stirring of vocations to the priesthood and the religious life, and his attempt to live a disciplined prayer life.

Significant episodes following upon his student years included his teaching at the Columbia Extension School and at St. Bonaventure College (1940–41); a pilgrimage to the shrine of Our Lady of Cobre in Cuba (1940); a private retreat during Holy Week and Easter at the Abbey of Our Lady of Gethsemani, a Cistercian foundation of the Strict Observance, near Bardstown, Kentucky (1941); and a brief period as a volunteer helper at Friendship House, a small lay community in Harlem (1941).

Merton presented himself for admission to the Abbey of Our Lady at Gethsemani (December 1941); was received into the novitiate and given the name of Louis in the religious life (1942); took simple vows (March 1944) and solemn vows (March 1947); and was ordained to the priesthood (May1949).

His skills as a writer and a linguist were recognized by his superiors, and he was used early in his years at Gethsemani in translating some of the classics of Cistercian life. The publication of early volumes of poetry (1944–49), together with the runaway success of his spiritual autobiography (*The Seven Storey Mountain*, 1948) secured for him a unique position in the life of the community.

Writing continued to dominate a good deal of his life and significant publications (especially *Seeds of Contemplation*, 1949, *The Sign of Jonas*, 1953, *Bread in the Wilderness*, 1953, *No Man Is an Island*, 1955) secured his reputation as a spiritual guide.

Merton also carried significant responsibilities within the community for teaching, training, and spiritual oversight as master of the scholastics (1951–55) and master of the novices (1955–65).

The 1950s also saw on Merton's part a great deal of restlessness: repeated questions about moving to another religious community, compulsive writing, endless correspondence, and tussles with Abbot James Fox and, in due course, with the censors of his order.

Merton was granted American citizenship in 1951, but it was in the late 1950s and the early 1960s that his wide-ranging mind and passionate concern about the world led him in his writing (books, articles, poetry, and letters) to voice prophetic concerns about the abuses of power, civil rights, the environment, nuclear weapons, Vietnam.

Merton gave up his work as Master of the Novices in 1965 and began to live full time at the hermitage, but he continued to give himself a good deal of latitude in his interpretation of what it meant to be a religious and a hermit, and not least of all during the spring and summer of 1966, which were dominated by his relationship with "M," the young student nurse who had cared for him in hospital.

Later publications included *Seeds of Destruction* (1964), *Raids on the Unspeakable* (1966), *Conjectures of a Guilty Bystander* (1966), and *Mystics and Zen Masters* (1967). Meanwhile, a Thomas Merton Room had been opened at Bellarmine College (1963), and the Merton Legacy Trust had been established with responsibility for his literary estate (1967).

Merton, who had developed links with scholars of several world faith communities from the mid-1950s, began to look increasingly for a recognition of the shared tradition of contemplative wisdom that belongs to men and women of faith in all the great religious allegiances.

Merton was encouraged by Abbot Flavian Burns to make an extensive journey to the East in the closing months of 1968, visiting India, Ceylon, Singapore, and Thailand, including meetings with the Dalai Lama (November 1968).

Merton gave a paper at a conference of religious in Bangkok, and it was there that he died soon after his lecture, having suffered electrocution and heart failure (10 December 1968). His body was returned for interment at Gethsemani.

Many of Merton's books, including his *Collected Poems*, were only published after his death: *Contemplative Prayer* (1969), *Contemplation in a World of Action* (1971), *The Asian Journal* (1973), *Love and Living* (1979), *The Non-Violent Alternative* (1980). The bulk of his *Letters* were published in five volumes (1985–94), and the seven volumes of his *Journals* were duly published (1995–98).

Thomas Merton, who had pursued parallel vocations throughout his religious life as a Trappist monk, a writer, a contemplative, a social critic and an ecumenist, has continued since the years following his death to speak to large numbers of people all over the world.

PART ONE

~ENCOUNTERING GOD~

Thomas Merton discovered at an early stage that the search for God and the search for his true self were deeply and inextricably bound up in one another. The themes that are brought together in this first section—"Encountering God," "Exploring the Depths," "Discerning the Truth," and "Finding My True Self"—lead inexorably into one another. What is so remarkable is the degree to which Merton engaged in his own personal story with all that these themes represent, and that he thereby became—albeit unwittingly—an inspiration to large numbers of people who in very different circumstances have found something of their story in his story. But there is something more: It is no less the case that these themes provide the backcloth to everything else that follows in this anthology. The challenge of living the Gospel, the call to the life of prayer, the engagement with the world, an awareness of the church's true vocation, and the mysteries of faith: all these can only be seen in the light of that Divine Passion—God's search for us and our search for God— which became the beginning and the end of Merton's journey.

Those who had known Merton during his earlier years might well have been surprised by the turn of events which enabled him to become a voice which continues to speak so powerfully and so passionately of the things of God. The traumas of childhood and adolescence, the early agnosticism, the spirit of something approaching self-destruction: All these gave way in due course to an abiding passion for God, for people, and for the questions with which he wrestled throughout his life. Reading, friendships, and the challenge and disciplines of Catholicism all played their part in his formation. But he was a man for whom there could be no half measures—"I want to give God everything"[1]—and so it was that he pursued in his life as a Trappist monk the most austere, the most rigorous, of all monastic vocations. But Merton, who was always so much larger than life, became not only a monk and a contemplative, but a writer with an international reputation, an outspoken social critic as the United States tore itself apart in the 1960s over civil rights, the arms race and Vietnam, and a pioneer in the field of interfaith dialogue.

Merton was also a man of contradictions. He was a deeply human man, down to earth, direct, and spontaneous in his dealings with people, a man of great personal charm with an inner freedom and a disarming friendliness. Those who knew him best recall the gaiety, the infectious humor, the belly laughter. But he could also be a restless spirit, questioning, provoking, pushing at the boundaries. Few men would have wanted to be his abbot! He was a free spirit; he could not be easily contained or constrained, but his discovery of God—or should that be God's discovery of him?—left him in no doubt about the divine initiative and the primacy of grace.

It may well be that Merton's emphasis upon the darkness that so often overwhelms those who persevere in the spiritual life owed something to his own personal psychology and to the insecurities of childhood and adolescence. Nonetheless, he saw that the vocation to the religious life is a call into the wilderness, and he spoke of himself at different times as a stranger, an alien, an exile, a pilgrim. But to explore the depths—personal and corporate, the things that belong to our deepest selves and the things that belong to the world of which we are a part—became in Merton's experience a penetration into the heart of darkness where God is to be found. He wrote of "a country of loneliness and of a kind of hunger,"[2] and he discerned in the darkness the truth that God "may be more present to us when He is absent than when He is present."[3] But one thing more: It was in the darkness, and especially in the life of contemplative prayer, that he found a deeper awareness of the world's needs. In entering the depths within, he was also entering the depths with others.

Merton spoke of the alienation that lies at the heart of the human condition. He brought a prophetic awareness, a prophetic voice, to the world and to the church, but he had first learned that such things are possible only where there is a deep identification with the pain of the world. It was for him part of the grace of transformation that the discontents that plagued him throughout his years at Gethsemani—and to which his *Journals* bear a powerful witness—constituted for him what might be best described as a field of energy within which one who was separated from the world might nevertheless find an openness and a profound empathy which enabled him to enter into the pain, the anguish, of the world.

The common experience of being "a perplexed and struggling race" does not necessarily obscure the realization that life must have meaning, even if the full meaning escapes us.[4] Merton laid great stress in his writings upon the freedom of the individual: freedom from the power of institutions, freedom from the mindset of a mass culture. The challenge is not, therefore, to look for a meaning that is imposed by God from the outside, which invariably means a predetermined pattern that others will all too readily impose, but rather to create *from within* by grace a meaning, a pattern of discipleship that is true to God and to ourselves.[5]

What Merton sought was an awareness of "the presence of God *in this present life*."[6] His abiding witness in his several vocations is that men and women might find their deepest freedom in God; and, holding firm to the central mystery of Christian faith, he acknowledged that "in order to become myself I must cease to be what I always thought I wanted to be.... and in order to live I have to die."[7] In his refusal to conform, to give way, to settle for a quiet life, he continues to encourage those who go beyond the conventions and the superficialities of life and dare to claim for themselves the freedom of the sons and daughters of God.

~Encountering God~

Reflection

Many of Thomas Merton's drawings are inspired by a rich heritage of religious art.

The circle, which has been employed by many traditions of faith to represent the totality, the unity, of the Godhead is pressed into service here, but the interconnected circles speak also of a dynamic Trinitarian faith in which ideas of movement, of perpetual motion, are also captured and conveyed.

But could it be that the open spaces in the heart of Merton's "Three-Personed God"[1] speak also of the God who waits to receive into himself all that we are and hope to be?

It is not we who choose to awaken ourselves, but God who chooses to awaken us.[2]

ANTHOLOGY

The Divine Initiative

Our discovery of God is, in a way, God's discovery of us.[3]

——⚬⚬⚬——

The only One who can teach us to find God is God, Himself, Alone.[4]

——⚬⚬⚬——

It is not we who choose to awaken ourselves, but God Who chooses to awaken us.[5]

Our Deepest Freedom

Our encounter with God should be...the discovery of our own deepest freedom.[6]

——⚬⚬⚬——

Whether we are good or bad, wise or foolish, there is always this sudden irruption, this breakthrough of God's freedom into our life, turning the whole thing upside down so that it comes out, contrary to all expectation, right side up. This is grace, this is salvation, this is Christianity.[7]

The Transforming Presence

It is no longer I, but You who work and grow: It is your life, not mine that makes these new green blades in the transforming of my soul.[8]

——⚬⚬⚬——

God, who is everywhere, never leaves us. Yet, He seems sometimes to be present, sometimes absent. If we do not know Him well, we do not realise that He may be more present to us when He is absent than when He is present.[9]

——⚬⚬⚬——

Whether you understand or not, God loves you, is present in you, lives in you, dwells in you, calls you, saves you, and offers you an understanding and light which are like nothing you ever found in books or heard in sermons.[10]

Letting Go

Only when we are able to "let go" of everything within us, all desire to see, to know, to taste and to experience the presence of God, do we truly become able to experience that presence.[11]

Every man at some point in his life encounters God, and many who are not Christians have responded to God better than Christians.[12]

God gives Himself to those who give themselves to Him.[13]

Moving On

The moment we have found Him, He is already gone![14]

~EXPLORING THE DEPTHS~

REFLECTION

The experience of encountering God will vary from person to person, but this journey of discovery will invariably include some exploration of the depths within God and within ourselves. Catherine of Siena found it helpful to picture God the Holy Trinity as "an abyss, a deep sea,"[1] and Merton was in no doubt that "the way to God lies through deep darkness."[2]

But everything is held within the embrace of God's indestructible love and life, and it is possible to trace in this drawing the form of the dove who moved over the face of the deep, and who—even today—continues to move over the face of the deepest waters in God's continuing work of searching, testing, drawing out, and moving beyond.

───✸───

Our mind swims in the air of an understanding, a reality that is dark and serious and includes in itself everything.[3]

ANTHOLOGY

Entering the Darkness

The way to God lies through deep darkness.[4]

⸺❀⸺

It is in the deepest darkness that we must fully possess God on earth.[5]

⸺❀⸺

It is not so much that we come through darkness to light, as that the darkness itself is light.[6]

Knowing and Not Knowing

No mind can comprehend God's reality, as it is in itself, and if we approach Him we must advance not only by knowing but by not-knowing. We must seek to communicate with Him, not only by words, but above all by silence, in which there is only the One Word, and the One Word is infinite Love and endless silence.[7]

⸺❀⸺

We have to come face to face with the absence of God. There are various refuges...they may be inhabited, we may stay with them, but we have to know that they are not where we have to go. In the end, if we are fortunate, we will come to a point where there is a wilderness, an emptiness, and no way forward. Here we have to trust and allow ourselves to be found in God and to be content with that.[8]

⸺❀⸺

A door opens in the centre of our being and we seem to fall through it into immense depths which, although they are infinite, are all accessible to us; all eternity seems to have become ours in this one placid and breathless contact. God touches us with a touch that is emptiness and empties us. All variety, all complexity, all paradox, all multiplicity cease. Our mind swims in the air of an understanding, a reality that is dark and serene and includes in itself everything. Nothing more is desired...you feel as if you were at last fully born. All that went before was a mistake, a fumbling preparation for birth...And yet now you have become nothing, you have sunk to the centre of your own poverty, and there you have felt the doors fly open into infinite freedom, into a wealth which is perfect because none of it is yours, and yet it all belongs to you.[9]

The Interior Journey

Our real journey in life is interior: it is a matter of growth, deepening, and of an ever greater surrender to the creative action of love and grace in our hearts. Never was it more necessary for us to respond to that action.[10]

To seek God is to seek reality. And this must be something more than a flight from images to ideas. The interior life is not merely what is *not* exterior.[11]

There is a silent self within us whose presence is disturbing precisely because it is so silent: it *can't* be spoken.... Now let us frankly face the fact that our culture is one which is geared in many ways to help us evade any need to face this inner, silent self. We live in a state of constant semi-attention to the sound of voices, music, traffic.... We are not fully *present* and not entirely absent; not fully withdrawn, yet not completely available.... [But] the disquieting presence of our deep self keeps forcing its way almost to the surface of awareness.... With this inner self we have to come to terms *in silence*.... After all, it is in the depths of conscience that God speaks, and if we refuse to open up inside and look into those depths, we also refuse to confront the invisible God who is present within us. This refusal is a partial admission that we do not want God to be God any more than we want ourselves to be our true selves.[12]

The Secret Country

God is hidden within me. I find Him by hiding in the silence in which He is concealed.[13]

The secret country is a country of loneliness and of a kind of hunger, of silence, of perplexity, of waiting, of strange hopes: where men expect the impossible to be born but do not always dare to speak of their hopes.[14]

God seeks Himself in us, and the aridity and sorrow of our heart is the sorrow of God who is not known in us, who cannot find Himself in us because we do not dare to believe or trust the incredible truth that He could live in us, and live there out of choice, out of preference. But indeed we exist solely for this, to be the place He has chosen for His presence, His manifestation in the world, His epiphany.[15]

Into the Depths

The living God, the God Who is God and not a philosopher's abstraction, lies infinitely beyond the reach of anything our eyes can see or our minds can understand.[16]

It takes far more than courage to start out on a way that obviously leads to the far end of nothing, and to walk over the abyss of our own absurdity in order to be found and saved by God, who has called us to walk that way.[17]

God is present, and His thought is alive and awake in the fullness and depth and breadth of all the silences of the world.[18]

But oh God! Give us the generosity that will enable You to lead us into the depths.[19]

~DISCERNING THE TRUTH~

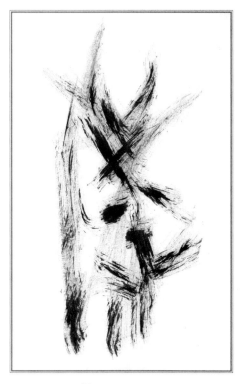

REFLECTION

No one knew better than Merton that the task of discerning the truth is a vocation for a lifetime—and beyond.

There is, however, nothing fixed, nothing static, and so it is that in this drawing with its simple brush strokes and the absence of any strong definition he captures something of the movement, the rhythm, the freedom of the dance of life. For Merton, encounter with God entails "the discovery of our own deepest freedom."[1] It is the freedom of the sons and daughters of God.

Not to seek Him as a possession, but to love Him and know Him and see Him as unknown and unpossessed.[2]

ANTHOLOGY

God in Us

Underlying Christianity is not simply a set of doctrines about God considered as dwelling remotely in heaven, and man struggling on earth, far from heaven, trying to appease a distant God by means of virtuous acts. On the contrary Christians themselves too often fail to realize that the infinite God is dwelling within them, so that He is in them and they are in Him. They remain unaware of the presence of the infinite source of being right in the midst of the world and of men.[3]

I can say as a Christian…that I have often experienced the fact that the "moment of truth" in the Christian context is the encounter with the inscrutable word of God, the personal and living interpretation of the word of God when it is lived, when it breaks through by surprise into our own completely contemporary and personal existence.[4]

Life is, or should be, nothing but a struggle to seek truth: yet what we seek is really the truth that we already possess.[5]

Unknown and Unpossessed

Every one of us forms an idea of Christ that is limited and incomplete. It is cut according to our own measure. We tend to create for ourselves a Christ in our own image, a projection of our own aspirations, desires and ideals. We find in Him what we want to find. We make Him not only the incarnation of God but also the incarnation of the things we and our society and our part of society happen to live for.[6]

It is those who want to possess God who remain far from Him because they think He is far from them. Actually, they can possess all that God has given them and receive it with gratitude, and glorify Him, and have all things without possession. But there remains one thing more to be done. Not to seek Him as a possession, but to love Him and know Him and see Him as unknown and unpossessed. This is to have God beyond possession. This alone is the life of the children of God.[7]

Finding the Meaning

Our life, as individual persons and as members of a perplexed and struggling race, provokes us with the evidence that it must have meaning. Part of the meaning still escapes us. Yet our purpose in life is to discover this meaning, and live according to it.[8]

Yet am I sure that the meaning of my life is the meaning God intends for it. Does God impose a meaning on my life from the *outside*, through event, custom, routine, law, system, impact with others in society? Or am I called to *create from within*, with Him, with His grace, a meaning which reflects His truth and makes me His "word" spoken freely in my personal situation?[9]

Sometimes we see a kind of truth all at once, in a flash, in a whole.

But once this general figure has become our property...then by a series of minute, difficult, toilsome steps we begin to find out, separately, as if with great trouble, over and over again, things that are just *parts* of this same idea we already possess as a whole.

The process may take days—or years...But we never begin to understand the idea really well until this arduous and discouraging process is also under way. And in this, we are really living that idea, working it out in our lives, in the manner appropriate to our own sad contingent and temporal state where nothing is possessed but in scraps and pieces, imperfectly, successively.

Yet we always long to possess truth as it is eternally in God's Divine Mind.[10]

~FINDING MY TRUE SELF~

REFLECTION

Few ancient Christian signs have been as serviceable as the fish which, taking its meaning from the letters of the Greek word, left early disciples in no doubt about the heart of the Gospel: *Jesus Christ, Son of God, Savior.*

Merton used the fish as a subject for his drawings on many occasions, but this particular fish is larger than life. Powerful and purposeful, it seizes our attention.

It may well be that the true self is to be found in Christ, but with this particular fish to point the way, it is no wonder that Merton could write of traveling in God's strength, of swinging in the grasp of God's love, of running in his swift ways, until our lives, having become his life, we might sail or ride like an Express.[1]

My true identity lies hidden in God's call to my freedom and my response to Him.[2]

ANTHOLOGY

My True Identity

My true identity lies hidden in God's call to my freedom and my response to Him.[3]

⚬⚬⚬⚬

It's about time I woke up and started to be myself and be what God intended me to be.[4]

⚬⚬⚬⚬

Before we surrender ourselves we must become ourselves. For no one can give up what he does not possess.[5]

Starting Where We Are

In returning to God and to ourselves, we have to begin with what we actually are. We have to start from our alienated condition.[6]

⚬⚬⚬⚬

The discovery of Christ is never genuine if it is nothing but a flight from ourselves. On the contrary, it cannot be an escape. It must be a fulfilment. I cannot discover God in myself and myself in Him unless I have the courage to face myself exactly as I am, with all my limitations, and to accept others as they are with all their limitations.[7]

⚬⚬⚬⚬

Good Shepherd, You have a wild and crazy sheep in love with thorns and brambles. But please don't get tired of looking for me! I know You won't. For You have found me. All I have to do is stay found.[8]

⚬⚬⚬⚬

The source of all sorrow is the illusion that of ourselves we are anything but dust. God is all our joy, and in Him our dust can become splendour.[9]

Finding the True Self

If we have no silence, God is not heard in our music. If we have no rest, God does not bless our work. If we twist our lives out of shape in order to fill every corner of them with action and experience, God will silently withdraw from our hearts and leave us empty.[10]

In order to become myself I must cease to be what I always thought I wanted to be, and in order to find myself I must go out of myself, and in order to live I have to die.[11]

We become ourselves by dying to ourselves. We gain only what we give up, and if we give up everything we gain everything. We cannot find ourselves within ourselves, but only in others, yet at the same time before we can go out to others we must first find ourselves. We must forget ourselves in order to become truly conscious of who we are. The best way to love ourselves is to love others, yet we cannot love others unless we love ourselves, since it is written, "Thou shalt love thy neighbour as thyself."[12]

Being What We Are

Be still
Listen to the stones of the wall.
Be silent, they try
To speak your

Name.
Listen
To the living walls.
Who are you?
Who
Are you? Whose
Silence are you?

Do not
Think of what you are
Still less of
What you may one day be.
Rather
Be what you are.

O be still, while
You are still alive,
And all things live around you.
Speaking (I do not hear)
To your own being,
Speaking by the Unknown
That is in you and in themselves.

"I will try, like them
To be my own silence:
And this is difficult. The whole
World is secretly on fire. The stones
Burn, even the stones
They burn me. How can a man be still or
Listen to all things burning? How can he dare
To sit with them when
All their silence
Is on fire?"[13]

Discovering Myself in Discovering God
To be open to the nothingness which I am is to grasp the all, in whom I am![14]

—∞—

Therefore there is only one problem on which all my existence, my peace and my happiness depend: to discover myself in discovering God. If I find Him I will find myself, and if I find my true self I will find Him.[15]

<hr />

All that He gives me becomes, in some way my own self. What, then, is mine? He is mine. And what is His? I am His.[16]

PART TWO

~LIVING THE GOSPEL~

Thomas Merton spoke of himself towards the end of his life as a Christian existentialist.[1] It is certainly the case that, while his acquisitive mind was open to the insights of writers from many traditions and many disciplines, his great strength as a teacher and a spiritual guide lay in the degree to which he drew upon his own experience. It is perhaps this quality, together with the undoubted popularity of so much of his writing, that enabled one scholar to speak of him as "a people's theologian."[2]

Merton knew that Christianity, which is a way of life and not only a way of thought, has to be lived.[3] The call to embrace the Gospel might be likened to an entirely new kind of birth,[4] and it follows that the full meaning of the Christian message can only be discerned by those who aspire to live the Christian life.[5] For Merton, the challenge to live the Gospel could only mean a discipleship that is open, questioning, passionate and engaged. This is the type of discipleship that he has come to represent for large numbers of people. This was *for him* the only way in which he could begin to live the Gospel.

One of the many tributes paid to Merton after his death by one of his brothers at Gethsemani recognized the extent to which he understood "what I want to be, or what I would like to be, or what I'm trying to be, or what I've gone through, or what I'm coping with."[6] Merton never aspired to be a role model. He was far too well aware of his fallibilities. But he has proved himself well able to identify with the commonplace experiences of large numbers of people. He knew that faith means living with doubt, that siren voices disturb and divert, that confusion and conflict are inescapable, that the journey of faith involves travelling, even though we may not always know where we are going.

Faith is faith, and the mystery of faith requires Merton to put his readers on their guard against over-scrupulous attempts to define, to rationalize. A generation for whom the all too familiar images are often found to have lost their meaning and for whom "words have become gods"[7] needs to learn that only one thing matters: the desire to love God.[8] Scripture, tradition, prayer and the claims of conscience will all serve as armor for the fight, but the primary resources are faith, hope and love, together with the capacity to discern the God who makes himself known in all the circumstances of our daily lives.[9]

But *mystery* and *faith* can be slippery words, and Merton is mindful of the deceptions of dogma, of piety, and of any presentation of the Gospel that has been so informed and shaped by the dominant culture of earlier centuries that its cutting edge has been blunted. He is a man for questions rather than answers; he sets his face against "neat and simple ready-made solutions," and he asks for the courage—the intellectual courage, the moral courage—to be willing to start from scratch in thinking things out for himself.[10] It is, of course, an approach to living the Gospel that presupposes a high degree of self-emptying, of self-abandonment.

It is precisely here that we begin to see why the desert—and the desert tradition of spirituality—came to mean so much to Merton. Monasticism had been born in the desert, and Merton, as he learned to wait upon God in the darkness, came to see himself as "a pilgrim and an exile in life."[11] Few of his writings gave him greater delight than his collections of the stories and the sayings of the Desert Fathers.[12] It was there that he touched the heart of the Gospel message, the heart of the mysteries of faith, the heart of discipleship.

It is scarcely possible to separate Merton's exploration of the desert from his experience of contemplative prayer, as he found himself without the familiar landmarks to indicate the path that he must take. It required him "to remain in loneliness and isolation.... waiting upon God in darkness."[13] But the desert, which is not merely a place but a type of Christian experience, speaks of the many different situations in which people find themselves—even in the midst of our crowded cities—as they cope with the deserts of the mind and of the spirit which can overtake any one of us.

Merton takes his place, therefore, alongside a succession of writers and spiritual guides who in the course of the last century have recovered for the church some understanding of the priority of the desert as a place of abandonment, but also of revelation, of transformation. This rediscovery of the desert as an inescapable part of the journey for many Christian people stands in sharp contrast to the secularity of the prevailing culture with its strong emphasis upon self-affirmation and self-expression. Is it perhaps in the desert—and in all that the desert represents—that the church must learn again what it means to hold the faith in obscurity and in silence, living with its brokenness and its incompleteness, watching and waiting? Could it be that this will always be for large numbers of individual men and women of faith—as it undoubtedly was for Thomas Merton—one unavoidable element in what it means to live the Gospel?

There is nothing here, however, that is enclosed or self-contained. Few people have brought to their living of the Gospel a greater sense of our solidarity with one another. The desert was for Merton the seed-bed in which he came to understand the paradox of hope and the priority of love. Hope is a gift: a gift of God, a gift of grace, but it can only be received by those who—like their

Lord—go down into nothingness in order to receive it.[14] Only then can Christian faith become what it is meant to be: "a religion of dynamic change."[15]

Merton who comes down to us as a man of words—a man of many words—is nonetheless able to cut through the endless definitions and speak simply of love as "a certain special way of being alive."[16] The truth of the desert that is waiting to be found is *compassion*, and it is only then that "the thirsty land turns into springs of water, that the poor possess all things."[17] Love is our true identity,[18] and it is only love that is able to create a new world in Christ. To love is "to enter into life,"[19] but living the Gospel takes us far beyond notions of personal salvation. Love is not merely the key to a fuller understanding of ourselves but to the meaning of God's entire creation.[20]

~LIVING THE GOSPEL~

REFLECTION

No other sign or symbol could represent the challenge of living the Gospel like the cross can. It speaks of the central drama, the central mystery, of Christian faith and life.

But Merton's drawing has two great merits: first, in depicting a Celtic cross with its many resonances—ancient and contemporary—he captures something of the simplicity and the austerity of missionary endeavor in a far earlier age, and, secondly, because there is something incomplete, unfinished, about the drawing, it is impossible for anyone to say in advance what living the Gospel might actually entail. Life and faith and love are gloriously open.

I want to give God everything.[1]

ANTHOLOGY

Seeking and Being Found

We could not seek God unless He were seeking us. We may begin to seek Him in desolation, feeling nothing but His absence. But the mere fact that we seek Him proves that we have already found Him.[2]

In the end, no one can seek God unless he has already begun to find Him. No one can find God without having first been found by Him.[3]

A New Kind of Birth

What Jesus speaks of is an entirely new kind of birth. It is a birth which gives definitive meaning to life.[4]

To be born again is not to become somebody else, *but to become ourselves.*[5]

A Way of Life

Christianity is first of all a way of life, rather than a way of thought.[6]

It is only by living the Christian life that we come to understand the full meaning of the Christian message.[7]

Where Am I Going?

Strange things can happen in the mystery of one's vocation.[8]

I say I want to give up everything for God. With His grace, perhaps my whole life will be devoted to nothing more than finding out what those words mean.[9]

My Lord God
I have no idea where I am going.
I cannot see the road ahead of me
and I do not know for certain where it will end.
Nor do I know myself,
and the fact that I think I am following your will
does not mean that I am actually doing so.
But I believe
that the desire to please you
does in fact please you.
And I hope
that I have that desire in all that I am doing.
I hope I will never do anything apart from that desire.
And I know that if I do this
you will lead me by the right road,
though I may know nothing about it.
Therefore I will trust you always.
Though I may seem to be lost and in the shadow of death,
I will not fear,
for you are ever with me,
and will never leave me
to face my perils alone.[10]

A Particular Goal

I—and every other person in the world—*must* say: "I have my own special, peculiar destiny which no one else has had or ever will have. There exists for me a particular goal, a fulfillment which must be all my own.… Because my own individual destiny is a meeting, an encounter with God that He has destined for me alone. His glory in me will be to receive from me something He can never receive from anyone else."[11]

—⚬⚬⚬—

I want to give God everything.[12]

~THE MEANING OF FAITH~

REFLECTION

The image of the cross repeats itself, but in this drawing, it is a cross that is to be carried, to be moved forward. The direction of travel may be uncertain, but what other guarantee can be required beyond the knowledge that we are in the company of one who supports and sustains, sharing the journey with us and making it his own.

———✦———

In one sense we are always travelling, and travelling as if we did not know where we were going.[1]

ANTHOLOGY

The Nature of Faith

We believe, not because we want to *know*, but because we want to *be*.[2]

———✦———

The religion of our time, to be authentic, needs to be the kind that escapes practically all religious definition. Because there has been endless definition, endless verbalizing, and words have become gods. There are so many words that one cannot get to God as long as He is thought to be on the other side of the words.[3]

———✦———

There is no doubt that the conventional and well-worn images in which our relations with God and with Christ are expressed are sometimes irrelevant in the modern world.[4]

———✦———

We do not want to be beginners, but let us be convinced that we will never be anything else but beginners all our life.[5]

The Gifts of God

What I need most of all is the grace to really accept God as He gives Himself to me in every situation.[6]

———✦———

He gives His gifts to all, the Holy Father of Lights, our Lord, our Life, in darkness. Not all accept them. Not all, who want to accept them, know how. Not all who try to accept them are humble or patient enough to wait and *see* how to receive the gift so that it remains with them.[7]

Faith and Doubt

Faith means doubt. Faith is not the suppression of doubt. It is the overcoming of doubt, and you overcome doubt by going through it. The man of faith who has never experienced doubt is not a man of faith.[8]

My own peculiar task in my Church and in my world has been that of the solitary explorer who…is bound to search the existential depths of faith in its silences, its ambiguities, and in those certainties which lie deeper than the bottom of anxiety. In these depths there are no easy answers, no pat solutions to anything. It is a kind of submarine life in which faith sometimes mysteriously takes on the aspect of doubt when, in fact, one has to doubt and reject conventional and superstitious surrogates that have taken the place of faith. On this level, the division between Believer and Unbeliever ceases to be so crystal clear. It is not that some are all right and others all wrong: *all* are bound to seek in honest perplexity. Everybody is an Unbeliever more or less! Only when this fact is fully experienced, accepted and lived with, does one become fit to hear the simple message of the Gospel—or of any other religious teaching.[9]

Travelling in Darkness

What do I look for tomorrow? Light? No. It is safer to travel in darkness. What I need is the grace to cease making any kind of fuss over anything: travel in darkness and do God's will.[10]

In one sense we are always travelling, and travelling as if we did not know where we were going.

In another sense we have already arrived.[11]

I only desire one thing—to love God.[12]

~ARMOR FOR THE FIGHT~

REFLECTION

There is a "catch me if you can" quality about this drawing. The invitation is always to be caught up in the life of the Spirit, but who knows where we might find food for the journey or armor for the fight.

The *bird* and the *wind* speak of the presence of God and of his desire to provide all that is needful. Bird and wind can both be traced in this drawing. The Spirit of God might be encountered as wind unseen, as life-giving breath from on high, but the gift of God for the people of God is a sharing in the Divine Life. It is love's energy working love.[1]

What matters is.... simply God and freedom in His Spirit.[2]

ANTHOLOGY

Scripture and Tradition

Necessity of the Bible. More and more of it.[3]

———∞∞———

By the reading of Scripture I am so renewed that all nature seems renewed round me and with me. The sky seems to be more pure, a cooler blue, the trees a deeper green, light is sharper on the outlines of the forest and the hills and the whole world is charged with the glory of God and I feel fire and music in the earth under my feet.[4]

———∞∞———

Tradition, which is always old, is at the same time ever new because it is always reviving—born again in each new generation, to be lived and applied in a new and particular way...Tradition is creative. Always original, it always opens out new horizons for an old journey.[5]

The Light of Conscience

Conscience is the light by which we interpret the will of God in our own lives.[6]

———∞∞———

There is only one thing that is of any importance in your life. Call it fidelity to conscience, or to the inner voice, or to the Holy Spirit: but it involves a lot of struggle and no supineness and you probably won't get much encouragement from anybody.[7]

Revelation

God manifests Himself everywhere, in everything—in people and in things and in nature and in events.[8]

———∞∞———

To appreciate this, you've got to know that *revelation* is all around you all the time. Revelation expressing itself as beauty, truth, goodness, and especially love!... Creation is lit up with the numinous. Numinous: that's God saying Hi! And *faith* is the surrender to this great gift of love, life!... To be alive in creation.... Submit to it—not in the sense of passive resignation, but in acceptance and participation in being![9]

The Spiritual Life

Whose prayer made me first pray again to God to give me grace to pray?[10]

———❧———

Study plays an essential part in the life of prayer. The spiritual life needs strong intellectual foundations.[11]

———❧———

Prayer is the truest guarantee of personal freedom.[12]

———❧———

I know too that in spite of all contradictions there is a center and a strength to which I *always* can have access if I really desire it.[13]

———❧———

What matters is not spirituality, not religion, not perfection, not success or failure at this or that, but simply God, and freedom in His Spirit.[14]

A Deep Repentance

I experience in myself a deep need of conversion and penance—a deep repentance, a real sense of having erred, gone wrong, got lost—and needing to get back on the right path. Needing to pray for forgiveness. Sense of revolt at my own foolishness and triviality. Shame and amazement at the way I have trifled with life and grace—how could I be so utterly stupid! A real sense of being flawed and of needing immense help, pardon—to recover some capacity to love God.[15]

Dying to Self

The things we really need come to us only as gifts, and in order to receive them as gifts we have to be open. In order to be open we have to renounce ourselves, in a sense we have to *die* to our image of ourselves, our autonomy, our fixation upon our self-willed identity.[16]

Faith and Love

Religion is not a matter of extraordinary spiritual experiences and that rot. The most important thing is a really simple and solid living faith. I think the thing that matters for most people is simply to live in an atmosphere of reasonable and alert faith and love for God and for other people, and in that way everything gets quite soon to have a simple religious meaning.[17]

The Law of Love *is the deepest law of our nature.*[18]

~SIREN VOICES~

REFLECTION

How does the artist depict the sights and sounds that confuse and divert? Or the clash of loyalties that eat away at the heart of who we are and want to be? Or the seductive embrace of the false gods that smothers the claims of conscience?

In this drawing, Merton captures something of the babel of sounds that bears down upon us—clamoring for attention, imploring, deafening. The noisy brass and the loud cymbal could not penetrate our defenses more thoroughly than the sharp-edged voices that make a shipwreck of our faith.

There is nothing to live for but God, and I am still full of the orchestras that drown His voice.[1]

ANTHOLOGY

The Root of Our Troubles

The root of our troubles is that our habits of thought and the drives that proceed from them are basically idolatrous and mythical.... We imagine that we are of all generations the most enlightened, the most objective, the most scientific, the most progressive and the most humane....We worship ourselves in this image.[2]

Activity for Its Own Sake

We believe that for us there can be no peace except in a life filled up with movement and activity, with speech, news, communication, recreation, distraction. We seek the meaning of our life in activity for its own sake.[3]

There is nothing to live for but God, and I am still full of the orchestras that drown His voice.[4]

The Deceptions of Dogmatism

The cultural features which Christianity acquired from its acclimatization in Europe are not all necessarily Christian. Hence, Christianity sometimes presents the aspect of an intensely active, individualistic, ethical system, based on a body of dogmatic truths which tend to define God objectively and to give a clear, definitive explanation of His will and of His plans for the world. What remains for man is then to accept these various speculative descriptions and explanations, and to live an energetic, progressive, productive life full of uprightness and good works.[5]

One must get along without the security of neat and simple ready-made solutions. There are things one has to think out, all over again, for oneself.[6]

There is an optimism which cheapens Christianity and makes it absurd, empties it. It is a silly, petty optimism which consists in being secure because one knows the right answers.[7]

The Deceptions of Piety

Silence is therefore important even in the life of faith and in our deepest encounter with God. We cannot always be talking, praying in words, cajoling, reasoning, or keeping up a kind of devout background music. Much of our well-meant interior religious dialogue is, in fact, a smoke screen and an evasion. Much of it is simply self-reassurance and in the end is little better than self-justification. Instead of really meeting God in the nakedness of faith in which our inmost being is laid bare before Him, we act out an inner ritual that has no function but to allay anxiety.[8]

We think that anything that costs us is God's will. If we want something, we easily persuade ourselves that God wants it as soon as it requires a little suffering to get it. From this fallacy of making a fetish out of difficulties for their own sakes, we get into the most fantastic positions, and use ourselves up, not for God but for ourselves. And we think we have done great things for God just because we are worn out.[9]

One thing occurs to me: how foolish it would be to base your whole life, to base important decisions, *merely* on a feeling of interior peace, or on a vague sense of oneness with God, considered as an experience.... Seek only God's will—the Kingdom of God and His justice—and peace and all the rest will be added to you.[10]

Hearing and Not Hearing

We have to be very careful about asking God questions and then answering them ourselves and saying: "God answered."[11]

If God does not speak to you it is not your fault and it is not His fault, it is the fault of the whole mentality that creates the impression that He has to be constantly speaking to people. Those who are the loudest to affirm they hear Him are people not to be trusted.[12]

Leading the Spiritual Life

It is not complicated to lead the spiritual life. But it is difficult. We are blind, and subject to a thousand illusions. We must expect to be making mistakes almost all the time. We must be content to fall repeatedly and to begin again to try to deny ourselves, for the love of God.[13]

Once you become aware of yourself as seeker, you are lost. But if you are content to be lost you will be found without knowing it, precisely because you are lost, for you are, at last, nowhere.[14]

I think the chief reason why we have so little joy is that we take ourselves too seriously.[15]

THE DESERT

REFLECTION

Thomas Merton understood the importance of the desert both in the biblical tradition and in the story of the church. But he knew that the desert—for Jew and Christian and Muslim—is first and foremost a place of withdrawal, of testing, of discovery, of transformation.

The genius of this particular drawing lies for me in the remarkable degree to which Merton conveys both the expanse and the barrenness of the desert scene: "No road, no path, / No land marks / Show the way there."[1] But isn't that what it's all about? Losing and finding ourselves in God.

There is no wilderness so terrible, so beautiful, so arid and so fruitful as the wilderness of compassion.[2]

ANTHOLOGY

The Call of the Desert

In wide open desert

No road, no path,
No land marks
Show the way there.
You must go by the stars.

Few live there
Far apart
Out of one another's sight
True men of God:
Such a place
Suffers only those
Who have made up their minds.

There is great love among them
And love for any other
Who can get that far.[3]

It is truly God who is calling me into the desert. But this desert is
not necessarily a geographical one.[4]

I don't need to take a long journey in order to find the desert: the
desert is myself.[5]

Go up, go up! this desert is the door of heaven!
And it shall prove your frail soul's miracle!
Climb the safe mountain.[6]

A Place of Testing

Be content to remain in loneliness and isolation, dryness and
anguish, waiting upon God in darkness. Your inarticulate longing

for Him in the night of suffering will be your most eloquent prayer.[7]

———— ❧ ————

When we have had something to suffer, we might do something for the world.[8]

———— ❧ ————

The real desert is this: to face the real limitations of one's own existence and knowledge and not try to manipulate them or disguise them.[9]

———— ❧ ————

It is Christ in us who drives us through darkness to a light of which we have no conception and which can only be found by passing through apparent despair. Everything has to be tested. All relationships have to be tried. All loyalties have to pass through fire. Much has to be lost. Much in us has to be killed, even much that is best in us. But victory is certain. The Resurrection is the only light and with that light there is no error.[10]

A Time of Gifts

I went into the desert to receive
The keys of my deliverance
From image and from concept and from desire.
I learned not wrath but love,
Waiting in the darkness for the secret stranger
Who, like an inward fire,
Would try me in the crucibles of His unconquerable Law.[11]

———— ❧ ————

Go into the desert not to escape other men but in order to find them in God.[12]

———— ❧ ————

The desert becomes a paradise when it is accepted as desert. The desert can never be anything but a desert if we are trying to escape it. But once we fully accept it in union with the passion of Christ, it becomes a paradise.... This breakthrough into what you already have is only accomplished through the complete acceptance of the cross at some point. There is no way around it if we want a valid renewal.[13]

⸺⸺

What is my new desert? The name of it is *compassion*. There is no wilderness so terrible, so beautiful, so arid and so fruitful as the wilderness of compassion. It is the only desert that shall truly flourish like the lily. It shall become a pool, it shall bud forth and blossom and rejoice with joy. It is the desert of compassion that the thirsty land turns into springs of water, that the poor possess all things.[14]

An Everlasting Spring

O flaming Heart,
Unseen and unimagined in this wilderness,
You, You alone are real, and here I've found You.
Here will I love and praise You in a tongueless death,
Until my white devoted bones,
Long bleached and polished by the winds of this Sahara,
Relive at Your command,
Rise and unfold the flowers of their everlasting spring.[15]

~THE PARADOX OF HOPE~

REFLECTION

Is it possible that the face of the Man of Sorrows can speak of the paradox of hope?

Merton's reply would almost certainly have been that only such a man—one who has borne our griefs and carried our sorrows—is able to speak to the torments of our world.

Merton demands time and again that we return to the central mystery of Christian faith—life through death to life—because it is there *and only there* that we touch the ground of Christian hope.

The cry that rent the temple veil
And split the earth as deep as hell
And echoed through the universe,
Sounds, in bombardment, down to us.
There is no ear that has not heard
The deathless cry of murdered God.[1]

Hope then is a gift.... but to meet it we have to descend to nothingness.[2]

ANTHOLOGY

Christian Hope

Christian hope begins where every other hope stands frozen stiff.[3]

That's the meaning of *hope*...to trust in the ultimate goodness of creation. Hope doesn't mean an anticipation or expectation of a deliverance from an intolerable or oppressive situation or condition.... That's what most of us are doing most of the time: wanting something other than what is. As I said—true hope is trusting that what we have, where we are, and who we are is more than enough for us as creatures of God.[4]

If you exist, you exist in hope. To cease hoping is to cease existing. To hope, and to exist, is to have roots in God.[5]

We are saved by hope for that which we do not see and we wait for it with patience.[6]

The Frailty of Hope

On the surface I have my confusion. On a deeper level, desire and conflict. In the greatest depths, like a spring of pure water rising up in the flames of hell, is the smallness, the frailty of a hope that is, yet, never overwhelmed but continues strangely and inexplicably to nourish in the midst of apparent despair.[7]

The real hope, then, is not in something we think we can do, but in God who is making something good out of it in some way we cannot see. If we can do His will, we will be helping this process. But we will not necessarily know about it beforehand.[8]

The Paradox of Hope

Hope then is a gift. Like life, it is a gift from God, total, unexpected, incomprehensible, undeserved...but to meet it, we have to descend into nothingness.

It is the acceptance of life in the midst of death, not because we have courage, or light, or wisdom to accept, but because by some miracle the God of life Himself accepts to live, in us, at the very moment when we descend into death.[9]

As Christ said, the seed in the ground must die. To be a seed in the ground of one's very life is to dissolve in that ground in order to become fruitful. One disappears into Love, in order to "be Love."[10]

Dynamic Change

Anyone who has read the prophets and the New Testament with any attention recognizes that one of the most essential facts regarding Christianity is that, being a religion of love, it is also at the same time a religion of dynamic change.[11]

Christian hope is confidence...in the dynamism of unfailing love.[12]

~THE PRIORITY OF LOVE~

REFLECTION

Merton was a man of contradictions, but he understood at an early stage in the unfolding of his several vocations the priority, the *absolute priority* of love.

Drawings—like words—are well able to expound the meaning of love. A pencil, a crayon, a paint brush—in the right hands—can capture the vitality, the intensity of love. Certainly this drawing conveys the extravagance, the sheer exuberance, of love. It could almost serve as a commentary upon Thomas à Kempis's word that, "Love flies, runs, leaps for joy; it is free and unrestrained. Love gives all for all."[1]

───∽───

Love.... is a certain special way of being alive.[2]

ANTHOLOGY

Being Alive

Whether or not you claim to be interested in it, from the moment you are alive you are bound to be concerned with love, because love is not just something that happens to you: *it is a certain special way of being alive.*[3]

⸺❦⸺

There is only one thing to live for: love. There is only one unhappiness: not to love God. That is what pains me on these days of recollection, to see my own soul so full of movement and shadows and vanities, cross-currents of dry wind stirring up the dust and rubbish of desire.[4]

⸺❦⸺

Love is my true identity. Selflessness is my true self. Love is my true character. Love is my name.[5]

⸺❦⸺

Love is, in fact, an intensification of life, a completeness, a fullness, a wholeness of life. We do not live merely in order to vegetate through our days until we die. Nor do we live merely in order to take part in the routines of work and amusement that go on around us....We do not become fully human until we give ourselves to each other in love.[6]

A New World in Christ

The command to love creates a new world in Christ. To obey that command is not merely to carry out a routine duty; it is to enter into life and to continue in life.[7]

⸺❦⸺

Love is the key to the meaning of life. It is at the same time transformation in Christ and the discovery of Christ.[8]

⸺❦⸺

If I am to love my brother, I must somehow enter deep into the mystery of God's love for him.[9]

—❧—

Love then is not only our own salvation and the key to the meaning of our own existence, but it is also the key to the meaning of the entire creation of God.[10]

—❧—

All true love is a death and a resurrection in Christ. It has one imperious demand: that all individual members of Christ give themselves completely to one another and to the Church, lose themselves in the will of Christ and in the good of other men, in order to die to their own will and their own interests and "rise again" as other Christs.[11]

The Ground of All

Love is not a problem, not an answer to a question. Love knows no question. It is the ground of all, and questions arise only insofar as we are divided, absent, estranged, alienated from that ground.[12]

—❧—

Love is the revelation of our deepest personal meaning, value, identity.... Love, then, is a transforming power of almost mystical intensity that endows the lovers with qualities and capacities they never dreamed they could possess.... Love is not only a special way of being alive, it is the perfection of life. He who loves is more alive and more real than he was when he did not love.... Life looks completely different to him, and all his values change.[13]

—❧—

I am happy that I can at least want to love God. Perhaps that is all I've got, but it is already all that is essential. And He will take care of the rest.[14]

—❧—

But love laughs at the end of the world because love is the door to eternity, and he who loves is playing on the doorstep of eternity.[15]

PART THREE

~LEARNING TO PRAY~

Thomas Merton's discovery of prayer preceded his discovery of faith, and of the Catholic Church, and of his vocations to the priesthood and the religious life. His account of his visit to Rome shortly after his eighteenth birthday—and at a time when he was very mindful of his father who had died two years before—tells of the occasions when he began to pray not merely with his lips or his intellect or his imagination, but "out of the very roots of my life and of my being, and praying to the God I had never known."[1]

This experience was to be short-lived as Merton threw himself into the turmoil of university life, but he had stumbled upon the ancient truth that prayer is God's work in us. It is not we who pray to God. It is he who prays in us. Merton had found the grace to pray, and this early experience of prayer was to be rediscovered both in his later years as a student at Columbia as he embraced the disciplines of Catholic piety and during the years of monastic formation at the Abbey of Our Lady of Gethsemani as he began to realize his Trappist vocation.

Merton—given half a chance—would be the life and soul of any party. He could be the most ebullient of men with a ready wit and a mischievous good humor, but he was well able to lay aside his restless energy as he explored the life of prayer in solitude and in silence throughout the long years at Gethsemani. Flavian

Burns, who was Merton's last abbot, recalled in Merton a man who could be in chapel for a whole half hour without moving a muscle or doing anything,[2] and of his spending three hours in uninterrupted mental prayer every morning.[3]

Everything that Merton has to say about prayer presupposes the activity of the Holy Spirit, but there is no suggestion in his writings that prayer is something that just happens. He identifies the desire to pray—or, rather, the desire to find God—as the one essential requirement for those who would learn to pray,[4] but he goes on to plead the necessity of finding time to pray, of slowing down, of listening to what is happening around us.[5] Merton could speak out of his own experience of the intimacy of prayer, but he was unable to speak with glib words. He knew too well the confusions and the contradictions with which we live, and it was there—precisely there—in the midst of the struggle, in the midst of personal anguish, that prayer must put down its roots.[6] Only then can prayer inform our understanding of the world and transform our vision.[7]

Merton came to appreciate over the years "the absolute primacy and necessity of silent, hidden, poor, apparently fruitless prayer."[8] It is his word of encouragement, of consolation. He placed great emphasis upon coming to God in our emptiness and learning to wait upon him in silence. Indeed, he described his own prayer as "a kind of praise rising up out of the centre of Nothing and Silence."[9] But there is nothing here to discourage us, because the experience of prayer enables us to "discover what we already have.... to experience what we already possess."[10] That is the gift and the grace, but there are no short cuts. If we want a life of prayer, we shall only find it by praying.[11]

It must not be inferred, however, that Merton is merely offering a way of praying that only really belongs in the monastery. His guidelines are clear: "Learn how to pray in the streets or in the country. Know how to meditate.... when you are waiting for a bus or riding in a train."[12] These things may not be easily achieved, but let there be no doubt about the scale of the revolution that he is pleading for where our understanding of prayer is concerned. To pray is to engage with God and, therefore, to engage with life in its entirety.

But the depths within Merton cried out "for solitude and for God alone."[13] He valued the solitude and silence that he found in the old rare books vault at Gethsemani where he was permitted to write, in the woods that surrounded the abbey where he was able to walk without the intrusions of community life bearing down upon him, and in due course at the hermitage where he spent the last three years of his life. He was feeling after—and he encouraged his readers to feel after—a silence in which "we listen for the unexpected...[and] are open to what we do not yet know."[14] There is nothing here, however, which detaches the one who prays from the hard realities of daily life. There is a solidarity—a deeply human solidarity—about the life of prayer, which brings a new awareness of the world's needs. It is with a triumphant flourish that Merton can write, "The more we are alone the more we are together."[15]

Contemplation was the heartbeat of Merton's life, and it is as a contemplative that he is probably best known. His understanding of the need for interior solitude and interior silence enabled him to move towards a type of prayer that was "beyond-concept, beyond-thought, beyond-feeling."[16] He was concerned to affirm the importance of the contemplative dimension in our experience and to plead for a far greater contemplative orientation in the life of the church, but he set his face firmly against any idea of the contemplative life as "esoteric knowledge or experience."[17] Contemplative prayer was for him the means whereby he could discover a life of greater simplicity and inner freedom. Awareness, intuition, perception: these are the words that best capture what he was feeling after, and it was in the ordinary circumstances of life that he asked for the foundations to be laid for a life that is lived not merely for contemplation but for God.[18]

Merton knew that contemplation could not stand alone. He was aware of its limitations. It could not *by itself* build the new world for which we pray.[19] It was in the life of contemplative prayer that Merton found his prophetic awareness and his prophetic voice, but contemplation and action were both required. And yet the contemplative life has a necessary part to play in bringing men and women closer to God and, therefore, to one another.[20] The wheel turns full circle. The Spirit who draws us into the depths is also well able to lead us out with a renewed understanding and a deeper commitment because "the Christian life—and especially the contemplative life—is a continual discovery of Christ in unexpected places."[21]

~LEARNING TO PRAY~

REFLECTION

If the *Divine Passion* speaks of our encounters with God—tentative, partial, but hinting at so much more—then prayer can be seen as one of the many ways in which we seek and (very occasionally) find each other. It is not merely a question of praying because we are seeking God, but because he is also seeking us.

Indeed, this drawing with its suggestion of birds in flight speaks of the work of the Holy Spirit as we are drawn upwards and outwards in the life of prayer.

———

The activity of the Spirit within us becomes more and more important as we progress in the life of interior prayer.[1]

ANTHOLOGY

The Meaning of Prayer

Prayer means contact with the deepest reality of life.[2]

—∞∞∞—

Our interior prayer is simply the most intimate and personal way in which we seek the Face of God.[3]

—∞∞∞—

It is the will to pray that is the essence of prayer, and the desire to find God, to see Him and to love Him is the one thing that matters.[4]

—∞∞∞—

A theology of prayer has to be seen in the light of our destiny. What are we here for? What does God intend for His world and for the men He has placed in it? And since our destiny is fraught with conflict and contradiction and struggle and even confusion, a theology of prayer is something that must flower in the midst of this struggle and confusion and even personal anguish.[5]

Stopping to Pray

If only I could pray—and yet I can and I do pray.[6]

—∞∞∞—

The best way to pray is: stop. Let prayer pray within you, whether you know it or not.[7]

—∞∞∞—

The whole thing boils down to giving ourselves in prayer a chance to realize that we have what we seek. We don't have to rush after it. It is there all the time, and if we give it time it will make itself known to us.[8]

—∞∞∞—

If we really want prayer, we'll have to give it time. We must slow down to a human tempo and we'll begin to have time to listen.

And as soon as we listen to what's going on, things will begin to take shape by themselves. But for this we have to experience time in a new way.[9]

Moving Forward

People who only know how to think about God during fixed periods of the day will never get very far in the spiritual life.[10]

The activity of the Spirit within us becomes more and more important as we progress in the life of interior prayer.[11]

My own part is to keep quiet and wait and attend to Him, rest in His presence, as if the cloud in which I find Him obscurely were to be the vehicle, the ship that is to take me there. Desire nothing more than this contact with Him in obscurity, ask no questions, do not try to rush Him or urge Him on, have no opinions, choose no way of my own, be with Him and let Him do the rest.[12]

As a man is, so he prays.[13]

Transforming Our Vision

Prayer must penetrate and enliven every department of our life, including that which is most temporal and transient.[14]

Prayer does not blind us to the world, but it transforms our vision of the world, and makes us see it...in the light of God.[15]

~THE EXPERIENCE OF PRAYER~

REFLECTION

Our experience of prayer is invariably tentative and uncertain. We bring the preoccupations of our daily lives, but all too often, we are left with a jumble of words and pictures, of hopes and fears, of petitions that flash by as they lose themselves in the busyness of living.

Sister Wendy Beckett speaks of entering God's energy when we pray,[1] and something of what those words might mean is captured for me by this drawing. Could it be that the God who is all in all moves within the nerve endings of our fractured and disconnected prayers, enabling us to touch the rays we cannot see, to feel the light that seems to sing?[2]

Everything I touch is turned to prayer…for God is all in all.[3]

ANTHOLOGY

In the Presence of God

Let me seek, then, the gift of silence, and poverty, and solitude, where everything I touch is turned to prayer: where the sky is my prayer, the birds are my prayer, the wind in the trees is my prayer, for God is all in all.[4]

⎯⎯∞⎯⎯

I have a very simple way of prayer. It is centered entirely on attention to the presence of God and to His will and His love.... Yet it does not mean imagining anything or conceiving a precise image of God.... It is a matter of adoring Him as invisible and infinitely beyond our comprehension, and realizing Him as all.... There is in my heart this great thirst to recognize totally the nothingness of all that is not God. My prayer is then a kind of praise rising up out of the center of Nothing and Silence.... Such is my ordinary way of prayer, or meditation. It is not "thinking about" anything, but a direct seeking of the Face of the Invisible, which cannot be found unless we become lost in Him who is Invisible.[5]

⎯⎯∞⎯⎯

First of all our meditation should begin with the realization of our nothingness and helplessness in the presence of God. This need not be a mournful or discouraging experience. On the contrary, it can be deeply tranquil and joyful since it brings us in direct contact with the source of all joy and all life. But one reason why our meditation never gets started is perhaps that we never make this real, serious return to the center of our own nothingness before God.[6]

Start Praying

In prayer we discover what we already have. You start where you are and you deepen what you already have, and you realize that you are already there. We already have everything, but we don't know it and we don't experience it. Everything has been given to us in Christ. All we need is to experience what we already possess.[7]

⸺∞⸺

The great thing is prayer. Prayer itself. If you want a life of prayer, the way to get it is by praying.[8]

⸺∞⸺

There is no such thing as a kind of prayer in which you do absolutely nothing. If you are doing nothing you are not praying.[9]

⸺∞⸺

How I pray is breathe.[10]

Praising God

My own personal task is…basically to *praise* God out of an inner center of silence, gratitude, and "awareness." This can be realized in a life which apparently accomplishes nothing. Without centering on accomplishment or non-accomplishment, my task is simply the breathing of this gratitude from day to day, in simplicity, and for the rest turning my hand to whatever comes.[11]

Silent Prayer

Most of my own prayers are completely inarticulate. I walk around saying "Love!" Or I just mentally keep slipping the latch that yields my whole soul to Love. You might do that too, one way or another.[12]

⸺∞⸺

Learn how to meditate on paper. Drawing and writing are forms of meditation. Learn how to contemplate works of art. Learn how to pray in the streets or in the country. Know how to meditate not only when you have a book in your hand but when you are waiting for a bus or riding in a train.[13]

The Hidden Prayer

The more I see of it, the more I realize the absolute primacy and necessity of silent, hidden, poor, apparently fruitless prayer.[14]

~~~

There is an absolute need for the solitary, bare, dark, beyond-concept, beyond-thought, beyond-feeling type of prayer. Not of course for everybody. But unless that dimension is there in the Church somewhere, the whole caboodle lacks life and light and intelligence. It is a kind of hidden, secret, unknown stabilizer, and a compass too.[15]

~~~

Prayer and love are really learned in the hour when prayer becomes impossible and your heart turns to stone.[16]

~~~

I think progress in prayer comes from the Cross and humiliation and whatever makes us really experience our total poverty and nothingness.[17]

~~~

Sometimes prayer, meditation and contemplation are "death"—a kind of descent into our own nothingness, a recognition of helplessness, frustration, infidelity, confusion, ignorance.[18]

Intercession

In our dealings with God He is free and so are we. It's simply a need for me to express my love by praying for my friends; it's like embracing them. If you love another person, it's God's love being realized. One and the same love is reaching your friend through you, and you through your friend.[19]

A Perpetual Surrender

The deepest prayer at its nub is a perpetual surrender to God.[20]

~~~

What is the use of praying if at the very moment of prayer we have so little confidence in God that we are busy planning our own kind of answer to our prayer.[21]

Empty, silent, free, opening into nothing—a little point of nothing that alone is real. What do you ask? Nothing. What do you want? Nothing. Very quiet and dark. The Father. The Father.[22]

~SOLITUDE AND SILENCE~

REFLECTION

The simplicity of this drawing can be deceptive. Its meaning is not immediately apparent, but it asks that we might be still and find new ways of looking, of listening.

In his printmaking, Merton used the things to hand—in this instance stems of grass—to hint at the openness, the unknowing, that is required of all who would follow the path of solitude and silence.

I go before you into emptiness,
Raise strange suns for your new mornings,
Opening the windows
Of your innermost apartments.[1]

———

This is a country whose center is everywhere and whose circumference is nowhere. You do not find it by traveling but by standing still.[2]

ANTHOLOGY

True Solitude

The door to solitude opens only from the inside.[3]

The truest solitude is not something outside of you, not an absence of men or of sound around you; it is an abyss opening up in the center of your own soul.[4]

In reality, all men are solitary. Only most of them are so averse to being alone, or to feeling alone, that they do everything they can to forget their solitude.[5]

If a man can't be alone he doesn't know who he is.[6]

In the Ground of Life

Is it true to say that one goes into solitude to "get at the root of existence"? It would be better simply to say that in solitude one *is* at the root. He who is alone, and is conscious of what his solitude means, finds himself simply in the ground of life. He is "in Love." He is in love with all, with everyone, with everything.[7]

But the one who has been found by solitude, and invited to enter it, and has entered freely, falls into the desert the way a ripe fruit falls out of a tree. It does not matter what kind of desert it may be: in the midst of men or far from them. It is the one vast desert of emptiness which belongs to no one and to everyone. It is the place of silence where one word is spoken by God. And in that word are spoken both God Himself and all things.[8]

I come into solitude to hear the words of God.[9]

The man who has found solitude is empty, as if he had been emptied by death. He has advanced beyond all horizons. There are no directions left in which he can travel. This is a country whose center is everywhere and whose circumference is nowhere. You do not find it by traveling but by standing still.[10]

Tested by Silence

There should be at least a room, or some corner where no one will find you and disturb you or notice you. You should be able to untether yourself from the world and set yourself free, loosing all the fine strings and strands of tension that bind you, by sight, by sound, by thought, to the presence of other men.... Once you have found such a place, be content with it, and do not be disturbed if a good reason takes you out of it. Love it, and return to it as soon as you can, and do not be too quick to change it for another.[11]

The purest faith has to be tested by silence in which we listen for the unexpected, in which we are open to what we do not yet know, and in which we slowly and gradually prepare for the day when we will reach out to a new level of being with God.[12]

If nothing that can be seen can either be God or represent us to Him as He is, then to find God we must pass beyond everything that can be seen and enter into darkness. Since nothing that can be heard is God, to find Him we must enter into silence.[13]

Where is silence? Where is solitude? Where is Love? Ultimately, these cannot be found anywhere except in the ground of our own being.[14]

A Deepening Awareness

There is One Solitude in which all persons are at once together and alone.[15]

———∞∞∞———

The more we are alone with God, the more we are alone with one another.[16]

———∞∞∞———

Solitude has its own special work: a deepening of awareness that the world needs. A struggle against alienation. True solitude is deeply aware of the world's needs. It does not hold the world at arm's length.[17]

———∞∞∞———

The solitary, far from enclosing himself in himself, becomes every man. He dwells in the solitude, the poverty, the indigence of every man.[18]

———∞∞∞———

He is truly alone who is wide open to heaven and earth and closed to no one.[19]

———∞∞∞———

As soon as a man is fully disposed to be alone with God, he is alone with God no matter where he may be.

At that moment he sees that though he seems to be in the middle of his journey, he has already arrived at the end. For the life of grace on earth is the beginning of the life of glory. Although he is a traveller in time, he has opened his eyes for a moment, in eternity.[20]

~THE CONTEMPLATIVE VOCATION~

REFLECTION

Merton's vocation as a contemplative takes its place alongside his many other vocations, informing and deepening his awareness of God, and of himself, and of the world in which he found himself.

This drawing tells of the passion that draws us beyond the established patterns of orthodox piety, the words, the pictures, the images with which we so easily console ourselves. The contemplative might speak of being "sealed in the dark,"[1] but darkness and light are both to be found—in the solitude of the wilderness and in the pools of refreshment—as this vocation is realized and explored.

———

The contemplative life must provide an area, a space of liberty, of silence.[2]

ANTHOLOGY

The Gift of Awareness

Contemplation is a sudden gift of awareness, an awakening to the Real within all that is real.[3]

The contemplative is not just a man who sits under a tree with his legs crossed, or one who edifies himself with the answer to ultimate and spiritual problems. He is one who seeks to know the meaning of life not only with his head but with his whole being, by living it in depth and in purity, and thus uniting himself to the very Source of Life—a Source which is...too real to be contained satisfactorily inside any word or concept or name assigned by man.... Contemplation is the intuitive perception of life in its Source.... It is an obscure intuition of God Himself, and this intuition is a gift of God Who reveals Himself in His very hiddenness as One unknown.[4]

[Contemplative prayer is] *the coming into consciousness of what is already there.* God is so close![5]

A Way of Being

Let us remember that the contemplative life is first of all *life*, and life implies openness, growth, development.[6]

What needs to be made clear, however, is that contemplation is not a deepening of experience only, but a radical change in one's way of being and living.[7]

The important thing is not to live for contemplation but to live for God.[8]

We do not see God in contemplation—we *know* Him by love.[9]

The Crown of Life

But the active side of Christianity is nothing without the hidden, passive and contemplative aspect. Indeed, without the secret, interior, lowly, obscure knowledge of God in contemplation, the activity of the apostle is empty and fruitless.[10]

It is all wrong to imagine that in order to "contemplate" divine things, or what you will, it is necessary to abstain from every kind of action and enter into a kind of spiritual stillness where one waits for "something to happen." In actual fact, true contemplation is inseparable from life and from the dynamism of life—which includes work, creation, production, fruitfulness and above all *love*. Contemplation is not to be thought of as a separate department of life, cut off from all man's other interests and superseding them. It is the very fullness of a fully integrated life. It is the crown of life and of all life's activities.[11]

The contemplative life must provide an area, a space of liberty, of silence, in which possibilities are allowed to surface and new choices—beyond routine choice—become manifest. It should create a new experience of time...not a blank to be filled or an untouched space to be conquered and violated, but a space which can enjoy its own potentialities and hopes—and its own presence to itself. One's *own* time. But not dominated by one's ego and its demands. Hence open to others—*compassionate* time.[12]

The Ordinary Realities

It is very important in the contemplative life *not to over-emphasise the contemplation.* If we constantly over-emphasise those things to which access is inevitably quite rare, we overlook the ordinary authentic real experiences of everyday life as real things to enjoy, things to be happy about, things to praise God for. But the ordinary realities of everyday life, the faith and love with which we live our normal human lives, provide the foundation on which we build these higher things.[13]

Walking down a street, sweeping a floor, washing dishes, hoeing beans, reading a book, taking a stroll in the woods—all can be enriched with contemplation and with the obscure sense of the presence of God.... Such "walking with God" is one of the simplest and most secure ways of living a life of prayer, and one of the safest.[14]

The true contemplative is not less interested than others in normal life, not less concerned with what goes on in the world, but *more* interested, more concerned.[15]

The life of contemplation...is, then, a life of great simplicity and inner liberty. One is not seeking anything special or demanding any particular satisfaction. One is content with what is. One does what is to be done, and the more concrete it is, the better. One is not worried about the results of what is done. One is content to have good motives and not too anxious about making mistakes. In this way one can swim with the living stream of life and remain at every moment in contact with God, in the hiddenness and ordinariness of the present moment with its obvious task.[16]

Action and Contemplation

Contemplation is out of the question for anyone who does not try to cultivate compassion for other men.[17]

The closer the contemplative is to God, the closer he is to other men. The more he loves God, the more he can love the people he lives with. He does not withdraw from them to shake them off, to get away from, them, but in the truest sense to *find* them. *Omnes in Christo unum sumus*. (All are one in Christ).[18]

If we experience God in contemplation, we experience Him not for ourselves alone but also for others.[19]

The Christian life—and especially the contemplative life—is a continual discovery of Christ in new and unexpected places.[20]

Action and contemplation…become two aspects of the same thing. Action is charity looking outward to other men, and contemplation is charity drawn inward to its own divine source.[21]

Contemplation cannot construct a new world by itself. Contemplation does not feed the hungry; it does not clothe the naked; it does not teach the ignorant; and it does not return the sinner to peace, truth and union with God. But without contemplation…we cannot understand the significance of the world in which we must act. Without contemplation we remain small, limited, divided, partial: we adhere to the insufficient, permanently united to our narrow group and its interests, losing sight of justice and charity, seized by the passions of the moment… Without contemplation, without the intimate, silent, secret pursuit of truth through love, our action loses itself in the world and becomes dangerous.[22]

PART FOUR

~EMBRACING THE WORLD~

All that we know about Thomas Merton suggests that he would have embraced the world—passionately, critically—whatever his vocation had been. It was, however, his monastic calling which required him as he rediscovered the world to be so much more than a Trappist monk who was also a writer and a contemplative. The urgency of the times demanded the voice of a social critic who would speak *and continue to speak* to those who have ears to hear.

Merton's appetite for life, his generosity of spirit, his theological convictions and his political antennae served to ensure that he could not be indifferent to all that was happening in the world. His early concerns with questions of peace and justice as a student at Columbia in the mid-1930s gave way to his becoming, as a religious in the late 1950s and the 1960s, one of the most outspoken—some would say one of the most strident—critics in the United States as he threw himself into the debates regarding civil rights, nuclear weapons, and the war in Vietnam.

It is remarkable that Merton, who had withdrawn from the world to pursue his monastic vocation, should have been so alert to the events of his day. Wide reading and extensive correspondence with friends who became his eyes and his ears enabled him to be an informed and articulate critic, but it was the monastic perspective that he judged to be so important. It gave him the necessary degree of detachment, the independence of mind, the freedom to ask the penetrating questions. He was entirely persuaded that an age that might be described as "a time of crisis" required the insights of those who, having apparently left the world, are able nonetheless to plunge deep into the life of the world, listening to "the deepest and most neglected voices" that come out of the inner depths of our humanity.[1]

The much-related moment of illumination for Merton at the heart of the shopping district in Louisville—"at the corner of Fourth and Walnut"—had left him overwhelmed by a deep awareness of his solidarity with people: "that I loved all those people, that they were mine and I theirs, that we could not be alien to one another even though we were total strangers."[2] It was, however, a thoroughly hard-headed recognition of the realities of life that he brought to bear as he reflected on the hopes and fears, the faith and greed, the love and cruelty that determine the way in which we behave toward one another.[3] But his vocation was clear: it was nothing less than to see God and to embrace God in the whole world;[4] and for him, writing as a Christian, there was no conflict between choosing Christ or choosing the world. On the contrary, it was only in the light of his faith that he could find himself, the world, his brothers and sisters, and Christ.[5]

It was a global vision and a global ethic that Merton pursued, and nothing revealed these things more powerfully than the way in which he wrote about the natural world as he challenged the preconceived ideas of an earlier generation which had all too often taken the earth for granted and used the animal creation for its own pleasure and recreation. He rejoiced in the wonder and the diversity of nature, in the interdependence of all living things. For him, the world was utterly transparent, and God could be seen shining through.[6] There can be little doubt that Merton would have taken his place within a generation at the forefront of discussions about the environment. He challenged what he saw around him in the towns and in the countryside, taking serious account of the way in which we "deal death all around us *simply by the way we live.*[7] His challenge was that we might find an understanding of Christian obedience in today's technological society, which takes far more seriously our responsibility to God's creation.[8]

What gave a cutting edge to Merton's approach was his understanding of the importance of the present moment. Indeed, he looked back and traced the beginning of his own conversion to his awareness of "the presence of God *in this present life*, in the world and in myself."[9] The present moment is always in the biblical tradition a time of promise and a time of judgement, and so it is that Merton disdains the blandishments of both the past and the future and pleads instead for the qualities that the present requires: "openness, readiness, attention, courage to face risk." It was the possibilities, the challenges, presented by the present that had to be embraced in what Merton rightly saw to be a time of drastic change.[10] Few things mattered more as Merton's prophetic awareness enabled him to speak with a prophetic voice.

There is something unashamedly apocalyptic in Merton's writings as he speaks of a world in turmoil with humankind "sitting on a thin crust above an immense lake of molten lava."[11] He identifies the inner contradictions, the chaotic forces, within ourselves, and—fifty years after his death—he remains profoundly pertinent as he depicts our living in "an age of universal alienation and mass movements."[12] There was no doubt in his mind that we are living in "prophetic and eschatological times"[13] where any religious interpretation of life receives short shrift, and yet—a sign of hope—he points to the growth of "a truly universal consciousness."[14] For the Christian, what is required is the resolve to claim the freedom that is inseparable from the Gospel—not freedom from our obligations to the natural world or to one another, but freedom from the myths, idolatries, and confusions of a world that has lost its bearings.[15]

Few matters concerned Merton more in his later years than the violence that he observed wherever he turned. He spoke of humankind's "fatal addiction to war,"[16] and he feared for a world in which "slaughter, violence, revolution, the annihilation of enemies, the extermination of entire populations and even genocide *have become a way of life.*"[17] It is certainly easy to identify with Merton's cry from the heart, "Will there never be any peace on earth in our lifetime? Will they never do anything but kill, and then kill some more?"[18] Commentators have rightly drawn attention to Merton's tendency to oversimplify when he addresses questions of peacemaking, but he pleaded passionately for an acceptance of nonviolence as a living alternative, and none will dissent from his assertion that we have the power within ourselves as a race to make a difference. The problem can only be solved in the minds and hearts of men and women—*or not at all.*[19]

It is here that Merton's Christian faith comes centerstage. He rejoiced in our common humanity, but the humanism for which he pleaded requires deep roots in the God who in becoming man has shown us that our fellow man—brother or stranger, friend or foe—*is Christ.*[20] The message is unequivocal: "We don't really find out who we are until we find ourselves in Christ and in relation to one another."[21] Over and against the universal experience of alienation in its many forms, Merton sets the challenge to see ourselves as members of a race intended by God to be one organism, one body.[22.]

EMBRACING THE WORLD

REFLECTION

Thomas Merton does not ask that we look for interpretations or hidden meanings in his drawings. He is far more concerned that we shall learn to stop and be still and find a different perspective, perhaps even an entirely new way of looking at life.

It might be convenient in an anthology of his words and drawings to bring together some drawings and some themes so that they speak to one another, but it must not then surprise us if we find that a particular drawing might be used in different ways.

But what is being depicted in this drawing? Is it God going out to embrace his world with shafts of light and love? Or is it the world—with its own dynamic—rejoicing in its freedom? Does the speckled surface speak of the depths of the divine life, or of the physical geography of the planet that we inhabit?

We've learned a good deal in recent generations about an open, dynamic and expanding universe. Could it be that our images of God need to speak far more readily of the immensity of God if we are to hear and respond to the call to embrace the whole world?

I must see and embrace God in the whole world.[1]

ANTHOLOGY

Choosing the World

To choose the world...is first of all an acceptance of a task and a vocation in the world, in history and in time. In my time, which is the present. To choose the world is to choose to do the work I am capable of doing, in collaboration with my brother, to make the world better, more free, more just, more livable, more human.[2]

The "world" is not just a physical space traversed by jet planes and full of people running in all directions. It is a complex of responsibilities and options made out of the loves, the hates, the fears, the joys, the hopes, the greed, the cruelty, the kindness, the faith, the trust, the suspicion of all.[3]

We must begin by frankly admitting that the first place in which to go looking for the world is not outside us but in ourselves. We *are* the world. In the deepest ground of our being we remain in metaphysical contact with the whole of that creation in which we are only small parts. Through our senses and our minds, our loves, needs, and desires, we are implicated, without possibility of evasion, in the world of matter and of men, of things and of persons, which not only affect us and change our lives but are also affected and changed by us.[4]

Christ and the World

Do we really choose between the world and Christ as between two conflicting realities absolutely opposed? Or do we choose Christ *by choosing the world as it really is in Him, that is to say created and redeemed by Him, and encountered in the ground of our own personal freedom and of our love?* Do we really renounce ourselves and the world in order to find Christ, or do we renounce our alienated and false selves in order to choose our own deepest truth in choosing both the world and Christ at the same time? If the deepest ground of my being is love, then in that very love itself and nowhere else will I find myself, *and* the world, *and* my brother *and* Christ. It is not a question of either/or but of all-in-one.[5]

The Church and the World

There is in Christianity, or Christendom, and in Buddhism, and in many other religions, a tradition of *contemptus mundi* which needs to be re-examined and understood. Originally, no doubt, it was intended to give the believer a certain freedom of action, a distance, a detachment, a liberation from care without which any question of love for the people in the world would be completely irrelevant.... [But] contempt for the world became not contempt for the objectives of the world, but competition with the world on its own ground and for the same power, with contempt for its motives.[6]

———⊶⊷———

Christianity is suffering a crisis of identity and authenticity, and is being judged by the ability of Christians themselves to abandon unauthentic, anachronistic images and securities, in order to find a new place in the world by a new evaluation of the world and a new commitment in it.[7]

The Inscrutable Judgement of God

The Christian faith enables, or should enable, a man to stand back from society and its institutions and realize that they all stand under the inscrutable judgement of God and that therefore we can never give an unreserved assent to the policies, the programs and the organizations of men, or to "official" interpretations of the historic process.... The policies of men contain within themselves the judgement and doom of God upon their society, and when the Church identifies her policies with theirs, she too is judged with them.[8]

Taking Responsibility for Our World

People seem exhausted with the labor of coping with the complications of this world we live in. Yet it is absolutely necessary that we do so. We have got to take responsibility for it, we have got to try to solve the problems of our own countries while at the same time recognizing our higher responsibility to the whole human race.[9]

Even though one may not be able to halt the race toward death, one must nevertheless *choose life*, and the things that favor life. This means respect for every living thing, but especially for every man made in the image of God. Respect for man even in his blindness and in his confusion, even when he may do evil. For we must see that the meaning of man has been totally changed by the Crucifixion: every man is Christ on the Cross, whether he realizes it or not. But we, if we are Christians, must learn to realize it.[10]

Against the mass brutality of war and police oppression, solidarity with the victims of that oppression. Against the inhumanity of organized affluence, solidarity with those who are excluded from any participation in the benefits of almost unlimited plenty. Where "the world" means in fact "military power," "wealth," "greed," then the Christian remains against it. When the world means those who are concretely victims of these demonic abstractions (and even the rich and mighty are their victims too) then the Christian must be for it and in it and with it.[11]

One Human Family

Man is now not only a social being; his social nature transcends national and regional limits, and whether we like it or not, we must think in terms of one human family, one world.[12]

The progress of the person and the progress of society therefore go together.... The transformation of society begins with the person.... The Christian "giving" that is required of us is a full and intelligent participation in the life of our world.[13]

—⁂—

We must strive more and more to be universal in our interests and in our zeal for the glory of the One God.[14]

—⁂—

The more we are one with God, the more we are united with one another.[15]

—⁂—

I must see and embrace God in the whole world.[16]

DELIGHTING IN THE WHOLE CREATION

REFLECTION

Merton's love of the natural world dominated his waking hours. He needed no persuading that God had stamped his being, his undivided power, "In seed and root and blade and flower."[1]

Few people have felt as keenly as Merton the ancient insight that in the grit of earth we find the glory of heaven; and so it is— as he depicts the branch that bears not just its leaves but also the promise of new life—that he displays a sensitivity, a delicacy of touch, which enables us to see something of the immanence, the transparency, of God.

We are living in a world that is absolutely transparent, and God is shining through all the time.[2]

ANTHOLOGY

The Splendor of Creation

One of the most important—and most neglected—elements in the beginnings of the interior life is the ability to respond to reality, to see the value and the beauty in ordinary things, to come alive to the splendor that is all around us in the creatures of God.[3]

~∞~

Creation had been given to man as a clean window through which the light of God could shine into men's souls. Sun and moon, night and day, rain, the sea, the crops, the flowering tree, all these things were transparent. They spoke to man not of themselves only but of Him who made them.[4]

~∞~

A spring morning alone in the woods. Sunrise: the enormous yolk of energy spreading and spreading as if to take over the entire sky. After that: the ceremonies of the birds feeding in the wet grass. The meadowlark, feeding and singing. Then the quiet, totally silent, dry, sun-drenched mid-morning of spring, under the climbing sun.... It was hard to say Psalms. Attention would get carried away in the vast blue arc of the sky, trees, hills, grass, and all things. How absolutely central is the truth that we are first of all *part of nature* though we are a very special part, that which is conscious of God.[5]

~∞~

We are living in a world that is absolutely transparent, and God is shining through it all the time.... God manifests Himself every-where, in everything—in people and in things and in nature and in events and so forth.[6]

A Song Which God Is Singing

Today, Father, this blue sky lauds you. The delicate green and orange flowers of the tulip poplar tree praise you. The distant blue hills praise you, together with the sweet-smelling air that is full of brilliant light. The bickering flycatchers praise you with the lowing cattle and the quails that whistle over there. I too, Father, praise you, with all these my brothers, and they give voice to my own heart and to my own silence. We are all one silence and a diversity of voices.[7]

But now I am under the sky. The birds are all silent now except for some quiet bluebirds. But the frogs have begun singing their pleasure in all the waters and in the warm, green places where the sunshine is wonderful. Praise Christ, all you living creatures. For Him you and I were created. With every breath we love Him. My psalms fulfil your dim, unconscious song, O brothers in this wood.[8]

All creatures are like syllables in a song which God is singing. Everything that is, is just a little syllable in this song which God is continually singing.[9]

Man and Nature
The universe is my home and I am nothing if not part of it.[10]

The whole world itself, to religious thinkers, has always appeared as a transparent manifestation of the love of God, as a "paradise" of His wisdom, manifested in all His creatures, down to the tiniest, and in the most wonderful interrelationship between them. Man's vocation was to be in this cosmic creation, so to speak, as the eye in the body.... That is to say, man is at once a part of nature and he transcends it.[11]

How absolutely true, and how central a truth, that we are purely and simply *part of nature*, though we are the part which recognizes God.[12]

If you love God, you will respect His creatures, and respect all life because it comes from Him.[13]

All creation teaches us some way of prayer.[14]

Dealing Death All Around Us

Perhaps the most crucial aspect of Christian obedience to God today concerns the responsibility of the Christian in technological society toward God's creation and God's will for His creation.[15]

I have been shocked at a notice of a new book...on what is happening to birds as a result of the indiscriminate use of poisons (which do not kill all the insects they intend to kill). Someone will say: you worry about birds: why not worry about people? I worry about *both* birds and people. We are in the world and part of it and we are destroying everything because we are destroying ourselves, spiritually, morally and in every way. It is all part of the same sickness, and it all hangs together.[16]

What a miserable bundle of foolish idiots we are! We kill everything around us even when we think we love and respect nature and life. This sudden power to deal death all around us *simply by the way we live*, and in total "innocence" and ignorance, is by far the most disturbing symptom of our time.[17]

Our attitude toward nature is simply an extension of our attitude toward ourselves, and toward one another. We are free to be at peace with ourselves and others, and also with nature.[18]

Creation's Everlasting Secret

For, like a grain of fire
Smouldering in the heart of every living essence
God plants His undivided power—
Buries His thought too vast for worlds
In seed and root and blade and flower.

Until, in the amazing shadowlights
Of windy, cloudy April,
Surcharging the religious silence of the spring
Creation finds the pressure of its everlasting secret
Too terrible to bear.

Then every way we look, lo! rocks and trees
Pastures and hills and streams and birds and firmament
And our own souls within us flash, and shower us with light,
While the wild countryside, unknown, unvisited of men,
Bears sheaves of clean, transforming fire.

And then, oh then the written image, schooled in sacrifice,
The deep united threeness printed in our deepest being,
Shot by the brilliant syllable of such an intuition, turns within,
And plants that light far down into the heart of darkness and
oblivion
And plunges after to discover flame.[19]

~THE PRESENT MOMENT~

REFLECTION

It is the sharp edges that first capture our attention in this drawing, and this might so easily have been the way in which Merton would choose to convey the urgency that he felt about the present moment and all that it requires.

The drawing—whatever might have prompted it—speaks to me immediately of the porcupine whose coat of sharp spines or quills protects it against predators.

Merton understood the biblical witness that every moment is both a time of promise and a time of judgement. Could it be that "the courage to face risk" must therefore take its place alongside all the other necessary graces if some protection is to be secured against the heat of the battle?

———⊗⊗⊗———

What really matters is openness, readiness, attention, courage to face risk.... what you need is to recognise the possibilities and changes offered by the present moment.[1]

ANTHOLOGY

The Present Reality

There is no truth, no life, in an existence which refuses to face the realities of our time.[2]

⸺⸻⸺

Whatever is happening, is happening both with us and without us, in and beyond us.[3]

⸺⸻⸺

What is valuable is what is real, here and now. The present reality is the reflection of an eternal reality, and through the present we enter into eternity.[4]

The Presence of God

God was not for me a working hypothesis, to fill in gaps left open by a scientific world view. Nor was He a God enthroned somewhere in outer space. Nor did I ever feel any particular "need" for superficial religious routines merely to keep myself happy. I would even say that, like most modern men, I have not been much moved by the concept of "getting into heaven" after muddling through this present life. On the contrary, my conversion to Catholicism began with the realization of the presence of God *in this present life*, in the world and in myself, and that my task as Christian is to live in full and vital awareness of this ground of my being and of the world's being.[5]

Sinking into the Heart of the Present

The only essential is not an idea or an ideal: it is God Himself, Who cannot be found by weighing the present against the future or the past, but only by sinking into the heart of the present as it is.[6]

⸺⸻⸺

In a time of drastic change one can be too preoccupied with what is ending or too obsessed with what seems to be beginning. In either case one loses touch with the present and with its obscure but dynamic possibilities. What really matters is openness, readiness, attention, courage to face risk. You do not need to know precisely what is happening, or exactly where it is all going. What you need is to recognize the possibilities and challenges offered by the present moment, and to embrace them with courage, faith and hope.[7]

A Moment of Ultimate Choice

"Crisis" means "judgement," and the present is always being judged as it gives way to what was, yesterday, the future.[8]

You are not so much concerned with ethical principles and traditional answers to traditional questions, for many men have decided no longer to ask themselves these questions. Your main interest is not in formal answers or accurate definitions, but in difficult insights at a moment of human crisis. Such insights can hardly be either comforting or well defined: they are obscure and ironic. They cannot be translated into a program for solving all the problems of society, but they may perhaps enable a rare person here and there to come alive and be awake at a moment when wakefulness is desirable—a moment of ultimate choice, in which he finds himself challenged in the roots of his own existence.[9]

Confrontation with Christ

That is what it means to be a Christian: not simply one who believes certain reports about Christ, but one who lives in *a conscious confrontation with Christ* in himself and in other men.[10]

I am beginning to think that in our time we will correct almost nothing, and get almost nowhere: but if we can just prepare a compassionate and receptive soil for the future, we will have done a great work.[11]

Time and Eternity

Every minute life begins all over again.[12]

―――∞∞∞―――

Eternity is in the present. Eternity is in the palm of the hand. Eternity is a seed of fire, whose sudden roots break barriers that keep my heart from being an abyss.[13]

~THE PREVAILING SCENE~

REFLECTION

Few of Merton's drawings were given a title. This drawing is no exception, but it is one of half a dozen drawings—similar in concept, design and format—which are sometimes called *Jerusalem*.

It may be that Merton was attempting to give nothing more than an impression of the heart of the old city with its buildings standing cheek by jowl with one another, separated only by narrow passageways.

But few cities in the world can compete with Jerusalem if what the artist wants to portray is the disconnectedness of life, where self-contained communities impinge upon one another, and a spirit of deep fanaticism and fear permeates the whole of life.

And yet Jerusalem—the New Jerusalem—has entirely different connotations for men and women of faith, and serves to remind us that what we see is so much less than what might be.

———

We live in prophetic and eschatological times, and by and large everyone is asleep.[1]

ANTHOLOGY

A Huge Spontaneous Upheaval

We are living in the greatest revolution in history—a huge spontaneous upheaval of the entire human race...a deep elemental boiling over of all the inner contradictions that have ever been in man, a revelation of the chaotic forces inside everybody. This is not something we have chosen, nor is it something we are free to avoid.

This revolution is a profound spiritual crisis of the whole world, manifested largely in desperation, cynicism, violence, conflict, self-contradiction, ambivalence, fear and hope, doubt and belief, creation and destructiveness, progress and regression, obsessive attachments to images, idols, slogans, programs that only dull the general anguish for a moment until it bursts out everywhere in a still more acute and terrifying form.

We do not know if we are building a fabulously wonderful world or destroying all that we have ever had, all that we have achieved![2]

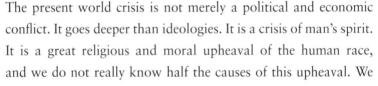

The present world crisis is not merely a political and economic conflict. It goes deeper than ideologies. It is a crisis of man's spirit. It is a great religious and moral upheaval of the human race, and we do not really know half the causes of this upheaval. We cannot pretend to have a full understanding of what is going on in ourselves and in our society.[3]

We are living in an absurd dream, and a very bad one. And it is the fruit of all sorts of things we ought not to have done. But the whole world is in turmoil, spiritually, morally, socially. We are sitting on a thin crust above an immense lake of molten lava that is stirring and ready to erupt.[4]

The Things That We Do

The things that we do, the things that make our news, the things that are contemporary, are abominations of superstitions, of idolatry, proceeding from minds that are full of myths, distortions, half-truths, prejudices, evasions, illusions, lies.... Ideas and conceptions that look good but aren't. Ideals that claim to be humane and prove themselves, in their effects, to be callous, cruel, cynical, sometimes even criminal.[5]

We are living in a society which for all its unquestionable advantages and all its fantastic ingenuity just does not seem able to provide people with lives that are fully human and fully real.[6]

We are living in an age of universal alienation and mass movements.[7]

The Time of No Room

We are living in the time of no room.... The time when everyone is obsessed with lack of time, lack of space, with saving time, conquering space, projecting into time and space the anguish produced within them by the technological furies of size, volume, quantity, speed, number, price, power and acceleration.

We are numbered in billions, and massed together, marshalled, numbered, marched here and there, taxed, drilled, armed, worked to the point of insensibility, dazed by information, drugged by entertainment, surfeited with everything, nauseated with the human race and with ourselves, nauseated with life.

As the end approaches, there is no room for nature. The cities crowd it off the face of the earth.

As the end approaches, there is no room for quiet. There is no room for solitude. There is no room for thought. There is no room for attention, for the awareness of our state.

In the time of the ultimate end, there is no room for man.[8]

The Storm of History

It is certainly true that the storm of history has arisen out of our own hearts. It has sprung unbidden out of the emptiness of technological man. It is the genie he has summoned out of the depths of his own confusion, this complacent sorcerer's apprentice who spends billions on weapons of destruction and space rockets when he cannot provide decent meals, shelter and clothing for two thirds of the human race.[9]

We of the West still hold instinctively to the prejudice that our world and our civilization are the "whole world" and that we have a mission to lead all others to the particular cultural goals we have set for ourselves. But the world is bigger than we think, and its directions are not always those that we ourselves have envisaged.[10]

The greatest sin of the European-Russian-American complex which we call "the West" (and this sin has spread its own way to China), is not only greed and cruelty, not only moral dishonesty and infidelity to truth, but above all *its unmitigated arrogance towards the rest of the human race.* Western civilization is now in full decline into barbarism (a barbarism that springs *from within itself*) because it has been guilty of a twofold disloyalty: to God and to Man.[11]

A Universal Consciousness

We are witnessing the growth of a truly universal consciousness in the modern world.[12]

In a world with a complicated economic structure like ours, it is no longer even a question of "my brother" being a citizen in the same country. From the moment the economy of another country is subservient to the business interests of my country I am responsible to those of the other country who are "in need."[13]

Questions and Answers

Obsolescence of a certain type of moral thought that deals *only* in absolutes, that makes no room for change and for provisional situations.[14]

I do not have clear answers to current questions. I do have questions, and, as a matter of fact, I think a man is known better by his questions than by his answers. To make known one's questions is, no doubt, to come out in the open oneself. I am not in the market for the ready-made and wholesale answers so easily volunteered by the public and I question nothing so much as the viability of public and popular answers, including some of those which claim to be most progressive.[15]

Eschatological Times

We live in prophetic and eschatological times, and by and large everyone is asleep. We realize it dimly, like sleepers who have turned off the alarm clock without quite waking up.[16]

Whether we like it or not, we have to admit we are already living in a post-Christian world, that is to say a world in which Christian ideals and attitudes are relegated more and more to the minority.[17]

We have lost our fundamentally religious view of reality, of being and of truth.... We have sacrificed the power to apprehend and respect what man is, what truth is, what love is, and have replaced them with a vague confusion of pragmatic notions about what can be done with this or that, what is permissible, what is feasible, how things can be used, irrespective of any definite meaning or finality contained in their very nature, expressing the truth and value of that nature.[18]

We live in a world in which, though we clutter it with our possessions, our projects, our exploitations, and our machinery, we ourselves are absent. Hence, we live in a world in which we say, "God is dead," and do so in a sense rightly, since we are no longer capable of experiencing the truth that we are completely rooted and grounded in His love.[19]

The Christ of Christian Freedom
In a word, "the world" feels no need of God either to explain itself or to be at peace with itself, or to regulate its activity.

Therefore, it seems to me, personally, that the basis of the Christian mission to the world is precisely that the Christian is "not of this world." He is first of all freed from its particular myths, idolatries, and confusions by his Christian faith. His first mission is to *live that freedom* in whatever way God gives him to live it.

The Christ he "preaches" (whether by word or silence) is the Christ of Christian freedom, Christian autonomy, Christian independence of the arrogant demands and claims of the world as illusion. Obviously the Christian is not "free" from the world as nature, as creation, nor is he free from human society. But he is free, or should be, from the psychic determinisms and obsessions and myths of a mendacious, greedy, lustful, and murderous "worldly" society—the society that is governed precisely by the love of money, and the unjust, arbitrary use of power.

What is important is to show those who *want to be free* where their freedom really lies![20]

Do not feel that the difficulties under which you labor are making your lives less significant. On the contrary, all Christians are everywhere in a kind of exile and it is necessary for all to realize this.[21]

The Cry of Faith

Where has it gone, this sense of the sacred, this awareness of the Holy? What has happened to us?[22]

⸎

Oh my God! You see what a barren and desolate place this world is—send us saints![23]

~VIOLENCE AND NONVIOLENCE~

REFLECTION

Few things preoccupied Merton more in the later years of his life than the violence that was endemic wherever he turned. He identified himself—as far as he could—with those who sought new ways, nonviolent ways, of resolving the tensions implicit in the fight for civil rights, the arms race, and the protest movement against American involvement in the war in Vietnam. But time and again, the response seemed to be, "There is no other way."

The horizontal lines placed so implacably upon the vertical in this drawing convey a similar message: There is no entry; no through road; no alternative. But Merton could not accept such a counsel of despair. He looked out upon "the winter of our hateful century"[1] and asked that we might begin to take responsibility for our world.

For the world to change, man must himself begin to change it, he must step forth and make a new kind of history.[2]

ANTHOLOGY

The Brutal Reality

We have got to face the fact that war is not merely the product of blind political forces, but of human choices, and if we are moving closer and closer to war, this is because that is what men are freely choosing to do. The brutal reality is that we seem to *prefer* destructive measures: not that we love war for its own sake, but because we are blindly and hopelessly involved in needs and attitudes that make war inevitable.[3]

⎯⎯ ∞ ⎯⎯

The human race today is like an alcoholic who knows that drink will destroy him and yet always has "good reasons" why he must continue drinking. Such is man in his fatal addiction to war. He is not really capable of seeing a constructive alternative to war.[4]

⎯⎯ ∞ ⎯⎯

There is hardly a nation on earth today that is not to some extent committed to a philosophy or to a mystique of violence.[5]

⎯⎯ ∞ ⎯⎯

John, in the might of his Apocalypse, could not foretell
Half of the story of our monstrous century,
In which the arm of your inexorable Son,
Bound, by His Truth, to disavow your intercession
For this wolf-world, this craven zoo,
Has bombed the doors of hell clean off their hinges,
And burst the cage of antichrist,
Starting with two great thunderbolts,
The chariots of Armageddon.[6]

Human Violence

Power has nothing to do with peace. The more men build up military power, the more they violate peace and destroy it.[7]

⎯⎯ ∞ ⎯⎯

The problem of racial conflict is part and parcel of the whole problem of human violence anyway, all the way up from the suppressed inarticulate hate feelings of interpersonal family and job conflicts to the question of the H-bomb and mass extermination. The problem is in ourselves. It is everybody's problem. The racial problem is only *one* symptom.[8]

Will there never be any peace on earth in our lifetime? Will they never do anything but kill, and then kill some more? Apparently they are caught in that impasse: the system is completely violent and involved in violence, and there is no way out but violence: and that leads only to more violence. Really—what is ahead but the apocalypse?[9]

Trying to Change the World

Wars are evil, but the people involved in them are good, and I can do nothing whatever for my own salvation or for the glory of God if I merely withdraw from the mess people are in and make an exhibition of myself and write a big book saying, "Look! I am different!" To do this is to die.[10]

What faces us all, Christians and non-Christians alike, is the titanic labor of trying to change the world from a camp of warring barbarians into a peaceful international community.[11]

If you love peace, then hate injustice, hate tyranny, hate greed—but hate these things *in yourself*, not in one another.[12]

Non-Violence

Nonviolence is not for power but for truth. It is not pragmatic but prophetic. It is not aimed at immediate political results, but at the manifestation of fundamental and crucially important truth. Nonviolence is not primarily the language of efficacy, but the language of *kairos*. It does not say, "We shall overcome" so much as "This is the day of the Lord, and whatever happens to us, *He* shall overcome."[13]

———— ◦◦◦ ————

The advantage of non-violence is that it lays claim to a *more Christian and more humane notion of what is possible.*[14]

Making a New Kind of History

Let us for the love of heaven wake up to the fact that our own minds are just as filled with dangerous power today as the nuclear bombs themselves. And let us be very careful how we unleash the pent-up forces in the minds of others.... *This problem is going to be solved in our thoughts, in our spirit* or not at all.[15]

———— ◦◦◦ ————

For the world to be changed, man must himself begin to change it, he must take the initiative, he must step forth and make a new kind of history. The change begins within himself.[16]

ON BEING HUMAN

REFLECTION

Merton rejoiced in his humanity with all its questions, conflicts, contradictions. But it was a humanity that could only be discovered and taken seriously into account if it is grounded in God.

Something of the darkness, of the pain and sorrow, of the world are represented by the darkness that bears down upon the scene in this drawing, but the large central capsule, which contains the seed of life, is set against the backcloth of the triangle—speaking unashamedly of the Triune God—which is thoroughly grounded, giving stability to the whole creation.

※

Guard the image of man for it is the image of God.[1]

Anthology

Our First Task

Our first task is to be fully human.[2]

Be human in this most inhuman of ages; guard the image of man for it is the image of God.[3]

The Human Predicament

This is simply the voice of a self-questioning human person who, like all his brothers, struggles to cope with turbulent, mysterious, demanding, exciting, frustrating, confused existence in which almost nothing is really predictable, in which most definitions, explanations and justifications become incredible even before they are uttered, in which people suffer together and are sometimes utterly beautiful, at other times impossibly pathetic. In which there is much that is frightening, in which almost everything public is patently phoney, and in which there is at the same time an immense ground of personal authenticity that is *right there* and so obvious that no one can talk about it and most cannot even believe that it is there.

I am in other words, a man in the modern world. In fact, I *am* the world just as you are.[4]

The Christian Calling

Our Christian calling does not make us superior to other men, does not entitle us to judge everyone and decide everything for everybody. We do not have answers to every social problem, and all conflicts have not been decided beforehand in favor of our side. Our job is to struggle along with everybody else and collaborate with them in the difficult, frustrating task of seeking a solution to common problems, which are entirely new and strange to us all.[5]

Conflict, Questioning, Searching

Paradoxically, I have found peace because I have always been dissatisfied. My moments of depression and despair turn out to be renewals, new beginnings.... So, then, this dissatisfaction...has helped me in fact to move freely and even gaily within the stream of life.[6]

⸮⸮⸮

What has been important above all has been living in the most meaningful possible way, at least for me. This has meant, again, a lot of conflict, questioning, searching.[7]

⸮⸮⸮

There is a time to listen, in the active life as everywhere else, and the better part of action is waiting, not knowing what next, and not having a glib answer.[8]

Living by and for Others

My life and my death are not purely and simply my own business. I live by and for others, and my death involves others.[9]

⸮⸮⸮

I must learn that my fellow man, just as he is, whether he is my friend or my enemy, my brother or a stranger from the other side of the world, whether he be wise or foolish, no matter what may be his limitations "is Christ."[10]

⸮⸮⸮

Conscience is the soul of freedom, its eyes, its energy, its life. Without conscience, freedom never knows what to do with itself.[11]

⸮⸮⸮

To say that I am made in the image of God is to say that love is the reason of my existence, for God is love.[12]

⸮⸮⸮

Everything that God wills in my life is directed to this double end: my perfection as part of a universal whole, and my perfection in myself as an individual person, made in God's image and likeness.[13]

Beyond All and in All Is God

Without God man becomes an insect, a worm in the wood, and even if he can fly, so what? There are flying ants. Even if a man flies all over the universe, he is still nothing but a flying ant until he recovers a human center and a human spirit in the depth of his own being.[14]

Either you look at the universe as a very poor creation out of which no one can make anything, or you look at your own life and your own part in the universe as infinitely rich, full of inexhaustible interest, opening out into infinite further possibilities for study and contemplation and interest and praise. Beyond all and in all is God.[15]

A CHRISTIAN HUMANISM

REFLECTION

It was through his understanding of Christ's Incarnation that Merton came to expound a Christian Humanism: "In becoming man, God became not only Jesus Christ, but also potentially every man and woman that ever existed."[1]

It is, of course, the word *potentially* that is so important, and it presupposes the work of the Holy Spirit—calling, enabling, equipping, directing. What this drawing captures, however, is the free play of the Spirit—moving where he wills—enabling us to see ourselves in relation to others who, like us, are caught up in the great dance of life.

———

God must be allowed the right to speak unpredictably. The Holy Spirit.... must always be like the wind in "blowing where He pleases."[2]

ANTHOLOGY

A Glorious Destiny

Ultimately there is no humanism without God.[3]

It is a glorious destiny to be a member of the human race, though it is a race dedicated to many absurdities and one which makes many terrible mistakes: yet, with all that, God Himself gloried in becoming a member of the human race. A member of the human race! To think that such a commonplace realization should suddenly seem like news that one holds the winning ticket in a cosmic sweepstake.

I have the immense joy of being *man*, a member of a race in which God Himself became incarnate. As if the sorrows and stupidities of the human condition could overwhelm me, now I realize what we all are. And if only everybody could realize this! But it cannot be explained. There is no way of telling people that they are all walking around shining like the sun.[4]

God and Man

God became man in Christ. In the becoming what I am He united me to Himself and made me His epiphany.... I am His mission to myself and through myself to all men. How can I see Him or receive Him if I despise or fear what I am—man? How can I love what I am—man—if I hate man in others?[5]

In becoming man, God became not only Jesus Christ, but also potentially every man and woman that ever existed. In Christ, God became not only "this" man, but also in a broader and more mystical sense, yet no less true, "every man."[6]

It is not a matter of *either* God *or* man, but of finding God by loving man, and discovering the true meaning of man in our love for God. Neither is possible without the other.[7]

The "word of the Cross"...gives the Christian a radically new consciousness of the meaning of his life and of his relationship with other men and with the world around him.[8]

We don't really find out who we are until we find ourselves in Christ and in relation to other people.[9]

Reaching Maturity

The Christian person reaches maturity with the realization that each one of us is indeed his "brother's keeper," and that if men are suffering and dying in Asia or Africa, other men in Europe and America are summoned to self-judgement before the bar of conscience to see whether in fact some choice or some neglect on their own part has had a part in this suffering and this dying, which otherwise may seem so strange and remote. For today the whole world is bound tightly together by economic, cultural and sociological ties which make us all to some extent responsible for what happens to others on the far side of the earth.[10]

My life is measured by my love of God, and that in turn is measured by my love for the least of His children: and that love is not an abstract benevolence: it must mean sharing their tribulation.[11]

But when you seek to affirm your unity by denying that you have anything to do with anyone else, by negating everyone else in the universe until you have come down to *you*: what is there left to affirm?

The true way is just the opposite: the more I am able to affirm others, to say "yes" to them in myself, by discovering them in myself and myself in them, the more real I am. I am fully real if my own heart says *yes* to *everyone*.[12]

The Stranger and the Alien

With those for whom there is no room, Christ is present in this world. He is mysteriously present in those for whom there seems to be nothing but the world at its worst.[13]

⎯⎯∞⎯⎯

It is my belief that we should not be too sure of having found Christ in ourselves until we have found himself also in the part of humanity that is most remote from our own.[14]

⎯⎯∞⎯⎯

God must be allowed the right to speak unpredictably. The Holy Spirit, the very voice of Divine Liberty, must always be like the wind in "blowing where He pleases"…but if we cannot see Him unexpectedly in the stranger and the alien, we will not understand Him even in the Church. We must find Him in our enemy, or we may lose Him even in our friend. We must find Him in the pagan or we will lose Him in our own selves, substituting for His living presence an empty abstraction. How can we reveal to others what we cannot discover in them ourselves?[15]

Belonging to God

We are in the same world as everybody else, the world of the bomb, the world of race hatred, the world of technology, the world of mass media, big business, revolution, and all the rest. We take a different attitude to all these things, for we belong to God. Yet so does everybody else belong to God. We just happen to be conscious of it, and to make a profession out of this conscious-ness. But does that entitle us to consider ourselves different, or even *better*, than others? The whole idea is preposterous.[16]

The Mystery of Christ

Only when we see ourselves in our true human context, as members of a race which is intended to be one organism and "one body," will we begin to understand the positive importance not only of the successes but of the failures and accidents in our lives. My successes are not my own. The way to them was prepared by others. The fruit of my labours is not my own: for I am preparing the way for the achievements of another. Nor are my failures my own. They may spring from the failure of another, but they are also compensated for by another's achievement. Therefore the meaning of my life is not to be looked for merely in the sum total of my own achievements. It is seen only in the complete integration of my achievements and failures with the achievements and failures of my own generation, and society, and time. It is seen, above all, in my integration in the mystery of Christ.[17]

PART FIVE

~THE CHURCH LOOKING BEYOND ITSELF~

Thomas Merton never called into question his faith in God or his commitment to Catholicism or his high doctrine of the church as the mystical body of Christ, but his strictures concerning the church, and especially the institutional life of the church, could be savage. He abhorred the bureaucracy, the triumphalism, the emphasis upon a rigid conformity. He looked out on a church that—from his standpoint—had lost its way in a world that had ceased for all practical purposes to be Christian. He spoke of living in a post-Christian age, of a "materialist neopaganism with a Christian veneer."[1]

The radical mind and heart that Merton brought to bear on so many contemporary concerns had ample scope when he reflected upon the situation in which the church found itself. The church had become a respectable institution—"a decorative symbol of the past"[2]—which failed to speak to him and to so many in his generation of change, of new life. It was, therefore, not merely the church but Christianity itself which had become identified with "the static preservation of outworn structures."[3] It was as if Christianity had been taken for granted for so long that people had forgotten its true meaning.[4] Merton's commitment to the priority of the present moment remained uncompromised, but he knew that while we live in the present, our responsibility must be to the future. He pleaded for a church that did not merely embody the past but actually embraced the future.

Merton's reading led him to see very clearly the diaspora situation in which the church was placed in the middle years of the twentieth century. Perhaps it was the desert tradition that enabled him to speak so positively about the challenge of being "Diaspora Christians" in an unashamedly secular society where the claims of religion are by and large unheeded.[5] But Merton wanted the church to find a truly Christian understanding of society, and it followed for him that the church—if it is to look beyond itself—must therefore be "a stumbling-block to the world, a sign of contradiction."[6]

Merton was feeling after a church that would be less of an organization and more of a community of persons united in freedom, in love, *and in Christ*. It was only then that the church might fully engage with the world in open dialogue and reason. He believed that this was the vision that lay behind Pope John XXIII's summoning of the Second Vatican Council. He watched as the Council's work unfolded and welcomed along the way Pope John's encyclical on peace and the Council's Pastoral Constitution on the Church in the Modern World as signs of a new beginning.

Freedom and love are the dominant themes in Merton's writing, both in relation to the church and also to the Kingdom of God, but there is nothing vacuous in his use of these large words. There was no place in his thinking for what he dismissed as "other-worldly aspirations and pious interiority."[7] Christians must do what they had always been required to do: build the Kingdom of God. The Trappist monk who spoke out of the depths of his contemplative prayer pleaded for Christians who would demonstrate the truth of the Gospel by lives committed to social action. Merton's faith—incarnational and eschatological—underscored his determination "to discover *all* the social implications of the Gospel."[8] The fault lines in society could be easily identified: poverty, discrimination, and racial and social injustice. But the initiative remained with God. He would build a new life and a new world, and Merton's prayer was that God might create them in and through us.[9] What Merton sought—and for him the Kingdom of God meant nothing less—was "a transformation of the world;"[10] and his points of reference as Christian men and women committed themselves to the task of building the Kingdom were the priority of God, the priority of the individual, the priority of freedom, and the priority of conscience.

Those who are familiar with Merton's story and his writings will know something of the degree to which his parallel vocations—as a Trappist monk, a writer, a contemplative, a social critic and an ecumenist—informed and challenged and enlarged each other. It can be seen in all that he has to say concerning the Kingdom of God, and it can be seen no less clearly in his encounters with the scholars, teachers, and spiritual guides of other faith communities. Nothing indicates more clearly Merton's prophetic imagination than his approach to the other great world faith communities. It was as though he had jumped a generation. He set his face against religious syncretism, but his reading—together with his correspondence with Jews, Muslims, Hindus and Buddhists—broadened his horizons beyond anything he could have anticipated at the outset. He spoke of "a whole new understanding of the Christian task in our time."[11] He sought a wider ecumenism in which a common inheritance of religious experience and contemplative wisdom might be explored.

Merton's experience had taught him that the great thinkers, together with the men and women of prayer in the various faith communities, had come to a knowledge of God and a love for God.[12] He was clear in his own mind that what he was looking for was nothing more than "the truth of Christ expressed in other terms."[13] Indeed, he had little doubt that Christ is to be found in those whom many might call unbelievers and that "this presence.... *is perhaps the deepest most cogent mystery of our time.*"[14] It may well be that it was Merton's awareness of himself as a stranger and an exile that enabled him to see the possibility—perhaps even the necessity—of finding God in "the *voice of the stranger.*"[15] But he had no illusions about the immensity of the task. Nothing would be achieved without humble and fraternal dialogue, and the work of dialogue could only be properly described as "a kind of arduous and unthanked pioneering."[16] What cannot not be ignored, however, is the way in which he spoke to a meeting attended by representatives of ten world religions in Calcutta six weeks before his death, emphasizing the unity that they already possessed and urging them to recover our original unity. "What we have to be is what we are."[17] A later generation, increasingly mindful of the capacity of religion to divide and destroy, might well judge that Merton's early and informal conversations in interfaith dialogue are not the least of his legacies to a fearful and tormented world.

THE CHURCH LOOKING
BEYOND ITSELF

The obscurity of history lies in the fact that its meaning is not always self-evident.

The disparate shades around the periphery of this particular drawing might well speak of a world struggling to understand.

God, represented by the great triangle, provides that necessary degree of openness through which some attempt might be made to identify the signs that point to an unknown future, and the Church, struggling to look beyond itself, begins to see that the future is yet to be written.

———⊸∞∞⊷———

The Church in this New World...must recognize the signs that point to the future, signs through which God speaks in the obscurity of history.[1]

ANTHOLOGY

The Church in the Modern World

We are no longer living in a Christian world.... Today, a non-Christian world still retains a few vestiges of Christian morality, a few formulas and clichés, which serve on appropriate occasions to adorn indignant editorials and speeches. But otherwise we witness deliberate campaigns to oppose and eliminate all education in Christian truth and morality.[2]

It is frightening to realize that the facade of Christianity which still generally survives has perhaps little or nothing behind it, and that what was once called "Christian society" is more purely and simply a materialistic neopaganism with a Christian veneer. And where the Christian veneer has been stripped off we see laid bare the awful vacuity of the mass-mind, without morality, without identity, without compassion, without sense, and rapidly reverting to tribalism and superstition.[3]

Changing Attitudes

We must adjust our attitude. We are living in a world that used to be Christian—and Hindu, Moslem, Buddhist. In the west we are in the post-Christian age—and all over the world it will soon be the same. The religions will be for the minority. The world as a whole is going to be not pagan but irreligious.

Hence we are already living, and will live more and more, in a world that we cannot look upon precisely as "ours" in any external and obvious sense. Certainly we shall "inherit the earth," but not to build an earthly kingdom in it, I am bold to think! Nor to have a genuinely Christian society in it, nor to have in any manifest way, an *accepted place* in it....We will certainly survive, but as genuine aliens and exiles. And perhaps this is as it should be.

It does not make one any less a Christian. On the contrary, it confirms me in my dependence on the Gospel message and in my dedication to Christ.[4]

A New Understanding

We have taken Christianity for granted for hundreds of years and now all of a sudden I think some of us are beginning to wake up to the fact that we have almost forgotten what it means, and that our ideas of God and His ways are far from corresponding to the actuality.[5]

⸺⸺

Christianity is no longer identified with newness and change, but only with the static preservation of outworn structures.[6]

⸺⸺

It is in a time like this that we are forced to have a Christian view of society at the risk of failing to be Christians altogether.[7]

⸺⸺

For many in our New World, the Church is merely a respectable institution closely linked to a past society.... Our responsibility is to the future not to the past.

The Church in this New World is more than a decorative symbol of the past. It is the mother of the future. Its members must open their eyes to the future; they must recognize the signs that point to the future, signs through which God speaks in the obscurity of history and in the present activity and life of the surrounding world.[8]

A Sign of Contradiction

I think the existence of the Christian in the modern world is going to be more and more marginal. We are going to be "Diaspora" Christians in a frankly secular and non-believing society.[9]

⸺⸺

The diaspora situation is one, then, in which the Church is a stumbling-block to the world, a sign of contradiction.[10]

Letting Christ Live in Us

The claim that "God is dead" is a claim that in the present state of grave religious crisis the old ways of talking about God and indeed of believing in Him no longer have any serious meaning for man.[11]

⸺∞⸺

We don't need so much to talk about God but to allow people to feel how God lives in us that's our work.[12]

~ON BUILDING THE KINGDOM OF GOD~

REFLECTION

This drawing is reminiscent of "The Present Moment" with its sense of movement and something of its sharp edges. But, of course, *the present moment* is where the Kingdom of God is to be built: here, now.

What shape or form the Kingdom might take in any one place or time has to be discovered. Only the advantage of hindsight can enable us to say, "Yes, God was in this place." Meanwhile *freedom* and *love* are to be the defining characteristics of our work in building the Kingdom. But one thing more: the drawing suggests a great explosion of energy, and we're brought back to the inescapable truth that God is the builder and founder of the Kingdom that endures.

I do not want to create merely for and by myself a new life and a new world, but I want God to create them in and through me.[1]

ANTHOLOGY

Freedom and Love

The task of the Christian in our time is the same as it has always been: to build the Kingdom of God in this world.[2]

—⁂—

To build the Kingdom of God is to build a society that is based entirely on freedom and love.[3]

—⁂—

Freedom from domination, freedom to live one's own spiritual life, freedom to seek the highest truth, unabashed by any human pressure or any collective demand, the ability to say one's own "yes" and one's own "no" and not merely to echo the "yes" and the "no" of state, party, corporation, army or system. This is inseparable from authentic religion.[4]

—⁂—

The Kingdom of God is the Kingdom of Love: but where freedom, justice, education, and a decent standard of living are not to be had in society, how can the Kingdom of Love be built in that society.[5]

Building a Better Society

The Christian cannot be fully what he is meant to be in the modern world, if he is not in some way interested in *building a better society* free of war, of racial and social injustice, of poverty, and of discrimination. It is no longer possible to evade this obligation by withdrawing into other-worldly aspirations and pious interiority unconcerned with human and historical problems.[6]

—⁂—

What is needed now is the Christian who manifests the truth of the Gospel in social action, with or without explanation. The more clearly his life manifests the teaching of Christ, the more salutary will it be. Clear and decisive Christian action explains itself and teaches in a way that words never can.[7]

To discover *all* the social implications of the Gospel not by studying them but by living them, and to unite myself explicitly with those who foresee and work for a social order—a transformation of the world—according to these principles: primacy of the *person*—(hence justice, liberty, against slavery, peace, control of technology etc.). Primacy of *wisdom and love* (hence against materialism, hedonism, pragmatism etc.).[8]

Taking Responsibility

It is only in assuming full responsibility for our world, for our lives and for ourselves that we can be said to live really for God.[9]

I do not want to create merely for and by myself a new life and a new world, but I want God to create them in and through me.[10]

The great historical event, the coming of the Kingdom, is made clear and is "realized" in proportion as Christians themselves live the life of the Kingdom in the circumstances of their own place and time.[11]

Built on Eternal Foundations

Men will indeed be of one tongue, and they will indeed build a city that will reach from earth to heaven. This new city will not be the tower of sin, but the City of God.

It will be a perfect city, built on eternal foundations, and it shall stand forever, because it is built by the thought and the silence and the wisdom and the power of God.

But you...and I are stones in the wall of the city. Let us run to find our places. Though we may run in the dark, our destiny is full of glory.[12]

~A WIDER ECUMENISM~

REFLECTION

Thomas Merton became increasingly aware of that universal tradition of contemplative wisdom shared by the world's great faith communities.

It was here that he found the unity of humankind—hideously obscured by the ignorance and folly of men and women with their absurd and self-indulgent claims to absolute truth.

The dark lines that move in all directions in this drawing speak all too readily of the forces of denial that crowd in upon us, but there is at the heart of our humanity the open invitation that God provides to discover the unity that we might possess.

We are already one. But we imagine that we are not. And what we have to recover is our original unity. What we have to be is what we are.[1]

Anthology

A Whole New Understanding

Strictly speaking, "ecumenism" concerns itself only with the "household of the "faith"; that is to say, with various Christian Churches. But there is a wider "oikoumene," the household and the spiritual family of man seeking the meaning of his life and its ultimate purpose.[2]

On every side there are new attitudes, especially in ecumenism. There is a whole new understanding of the Christian task in our time.[3]

The Ultimate Temptation

This...is the ultimate temptation of Christianity! To say that Christ has locked all the doors, has given one answer, settled everything and departed, leaving all life enclosed in the frightful consistency of a system outside of which there is seriousness and damnation, inside of which there is the intolerable flippancy of the saved—while nowhere is there any place left for the mystery of the divine mercy which alone is truly serious, and worthy of being taken seriously.[4]

The Breath of the Spirit

I will be a better Catholic, not if I can *refute* every shade of Protestantism, but if I can confirm the truth in it and still go further.

So, too, with the Muslims, the Hindus, the Buddhists, etc. This does not mean syncretism, indifferentism, the vapid and careless friendliness that accepts everything by thinking of nothing. There is much one cannot "affirm" and "accept," but first one must say "yes" where one really can.

If I affirm myself as a Catholic merely by denying all that is Muslim, Jewish, Protestant, Hindu, Buddhist, etc., in the end I will find there is not much left for me to affirm as a Catholic: and certainly no breath of the Spirit with which to affirm it.[5]

⁕

Whatever I seek in other traditions is only the truth of Christ expressed in other terms, rejecting all that is *really* contrary to His Truth.[6]

The Voice of the Stranger

How can one be in contact with the great thinkers and men of prayer of the various religions without recognizing that these men have known God and have loved Him because they recognized themselves loved by Him?[7]

⁕

God speaks, and God is to be heard, not only on Sinai, not only in my own heart, but in the *voice of the stranger.*

We must, then, see the truth in the stranger, and the truth we see must be a newly living truth, not just a projection of a dead conventional idea of our own—a projection of our own self upon the stranger.[8]

⁕

I honestly think that there *is* a presence of Christ to the unbeliever, especially in our day, and that this presence, which is not formally "religious" and which escapes definition...*is perhaps the deepest most cogent mystery of our time.* The Lord who speaks of freedom in the ground of our being still continues to speak to every man.[9]

A Truth That Is Shared

Christ is found not in loud and pompous declarations but in humble and fraternal dialogue. He is found less in a truth that is imposed than in a truth that is shared.

If I insist on giving you my truth, and never stop to receive your truth in return, then there can be no truth between us.[10]

Arduous and Unthanked Pioneering

I believe that the only really valid thing that can be accomplished in the direction of world peace and unity at the moment is the preparation of the way by the formation of men who, isolated, perhaps not accepted or understood by any "movement," are best able to unite in themselves and experience in their own lives all that is best and most true in the various great spiritual traditions. Such men can become as it were "sacraments" or signs of peace, at least. They can do much to open up the minds of their contemporaries to receive, in the future, new seeds of thought. Our task is one of very remote preparation, a kind of arduous and unthanked pioneering.[11]

Being What We Are

The deepest level of communication is not communication, but communion. It is wordless. It is beyond words, and it is beyond speech, and it is beyond concept. Not that we discover a new unity. My dear brothers, we are already one. But we imagine that we are not. And what we have to recover is our original unity. What we have to be is what we are.[12]

PART SIX

~ON BEING IN CHRIST~

Thomas Merton's journey to the Far East in the last two months of his life took him to Bangkok, Calcutta, New Delhi, the Himalayas, Ceylon, Singapore, and then back to Bangkok, where his journey was cut short by his tragic death on December 10, 1968. He had set out to give lectures in Calcutta and Bangkok, but—quite apart from additional invitations to speak in one place or another—he found that he was able to meet with monks, lamas, scholars, poets and artists from various traditions of faith. His three conversations with the Dalai Lama undoubtedly represented the most significant encounter of the whole journey, but it was while he was in India that he also spent some time in conversation with Chatral Rimpoche, a Tibetan Lama. It was exactly the kind of exchange that he had looked forward to as the two men talked about solitude, meditation, compassion, and perfection, and explored together various points where Buddhist and Christian insights might complement each other. Merton, writing in his journal, spoke of their complete understanding of each other as two people "who were *on the edge* of great realization and knew it and were trying, somehow or other, to go out and get lost in it."[1]

It is a marvelously evocative insight into a conversation in which two men from very different backgrounds and traditions of faith touched the depths of human aspiration, of religious experience. It could serve happily as a commentary on all that Merton had been feeling throughout his adult life as he sought the God Who *in Christ* had become "not only 'this' man, but also in a broader and more mystical sense.... 'every man.'"[2] Time and again we see Merton returning to the person of Jesus Christ, wrestling with all that the Incarnation might mean, and finding a new awareness of where Christian faith must lead. It was certainly an understanding of Christology which informed his global frame of reference as a social critic and an ecumenist. The boundaries of nationality, race, and religion were no longer serviceable. It was necessary to think in terms of our being "one human family, one world."[3] For Merton, to be in Christ was to be united—mystically, yes, but also politically, economically—with all humankind. "The more we are united to (Christ) in love, the more we are united in love to one another."[4] The mystery of our oneness in Christ could mean nothing less. The Asian journey enabled Merton to see something more of what these words might mean.

Merton had already discovered as he pursued his several vocations that the mysteries of faith have a dynamic quality. The great creedal statements concerning the mystery of God; or the incarnation, passion, death, and resurrection of Jesus Christ; or the transforming power of the Holy Spirit are not only theological propositions to which a pious assent might be given. Nor do they merely speak of events captured in the stories and pictures of faith. They tell rather of "a continuous dynamic of inner renewal."[5] But the cutting edge of Christian faith is to be found in the conviction that "Life in Christ is life in the mystery of the Cross."[6] It was in an early poem, written during his novitiate, that Merton captured something of what the mysteries of faith might mean: "If on Your Cross Your life and death and mine are one, / Love teaches me to read, in You, the rest of a new history."[7] In every area of his life's work, Merton was always reaching out and trying to see what the rest of a new history might look like, and what part God might play through him in realizing the potentialities locked up in every situation.

Life through death to life. It is a theme that repeats itself. Merton knew—no one better—that "a death struggle can also be a struggle for life, a new birth."[8] He had learned at an early stage that, "To find life we must die to life as we know it."[9] What mattered to him—the only thing that ultimately mattered—was union with God, and it was to that end that he pursued his monastic calling and all his related vocations with a single-minded devotion. He could be the most delightful of men, but he carried within him the wounds, the contradictions and the paradoxes which make him more impressive and not less impressive, more compelling and not less compelling. Nor did he always conceal the discontents that welled up from time to time. But he dared to believe that "underlying it all, in the deepest depths that we cannot possibly see, lies an ultimate ground in which all contradictions are united and all come out 'right.'"[10] Few men could be more engaging, and it may yet be that the contradictions and the discontents that are laid bare in his journals serve as his credentials to a world in which we struggle to come to terms with our own experience of disconnectedness, of fragmentation, of self-destruction. But for him "*on the edge* of great realization," there was only the desire "to go beyond everything…. and press forward to the End and to the Beginning, to the ever new Beginning that is without End."[11]

ON BEING IN CHRIST

REFLECTION

Small circles of light are separated from each other by the shade that defines their space. They stand in relation to each other but they do not overlap.

But Merton will not allow his readers to take refuge in a self-indulgent piety. It is not sufficient to plead that we are united to Christ. The words are meaningless unless we are united to one another.

Something of what that might mean is conveyed by Merton in his prose poem "Hagia Sophia," where the Christ who comes into the world is presented as "a vagrant, a destitute wanderer.... a homeless God, lost in the night.... a frail expendable exile."[1] Being in Christ takes on, then, a new frame of reference.

———

The more we are united to (Christ) in love the more we are united in love to one another.[2]

ANTHOLOGY

United in Christ

To be a Christian is then not only to believe in Christ, but to live in Christ and, in a mysterious way, to become united in Christ. This is both Christian life and Christian holiness.[3]

❦

Whatever I may have written, I think it can all be reduced in the end to this one root truth: that God calls human persons to union with Himself and with one another in Christ, in the Church which is His Mystical Body.[4]

❦

We cannot get too deep into the mystery of our oneness in Christ.[5]

The Word Made Flesh

Since the Word was made Flesh, God is in man, God is in *all men*. All men are to be seen and treated as Christ.[6]

❦

If God has become man, then no Christian is ever allowed to be indifferent to man's fate. Whoever believes that Christ is the Word made flesh believes that every man must in some sense be regarded as Christ. For all are at least potentially members of the Mystical Christ. Who can say with absolute certainty of any other man that Christ does not live in Him?[7]

Living in Christ

The more we are united to (Christ) in love the more we are united in love to one another.[8]

❦

When you and I become what we are really meant to be, we will discover not only that we love one another perfectly but that we are both living in Christ and Christ in us, and we are all One Christ. We will see that it is He Who loves in us.[9]

Life in Christ is life in the mystery of the Cross.[10]

Open to All Others

So in each one of us the Christian person is that which is fully open to all other persons, because ultimately all other persons are Christ.[11]

Christ suffers in the Church: and there is nothing suffered on earth that Christ Himself does not suffer. Everything that happens to the poor, the meek, the desolate, the mourners, the despised, happens to Christ.[12]

Finding Myself in Christ

There is no failure for those who are loved and sought by Christ. He loves you, even though you may feel that you have lost your religious energy and that your faith does not have its old drive. To feel oneself a great and vital Christian is a luxury that we have to do without today when God is so hidden and so unknown in His world.... Perhaps He wills to be hidden even in our lives. We must be content to be united with Jesus in His passion and in darkness, for it is thus that we cooperate with Him in helping others.[13]

I cannot hope to find myself anywhere except in Him.[14]

~THE MYSTERIES OF FAITH~

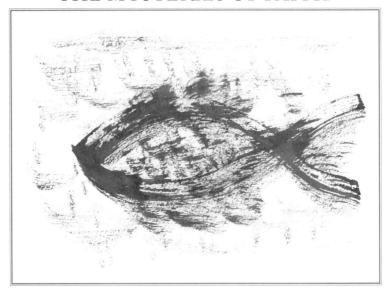

REFLECTION

The fish—one of Merton's several fish—makes a return appearance, but this drawing has a far clearer definition. The brush strokes give every suggestion of a purposeful moving forward. This is not a fish with a hidden message, a fish who merely points the way. This fish knows what it's about and where it's going.

So it is with the mysteries of faith, which are summarized for us in the great creedal statements of the church. They are not simply theological statements with their own appropriate liturgical observances. Christian faith cannot be distinguished from Christian living. The mysteries of faith are the stones by which we are to be built into a living temple, and central to faith and life—and to all the mysteries of faith—is the drama of death and resurrection.

———

Christ, the Incarnate Word, is the Book of Life in Whom we read God.[1]

Anthology

The Mystery of God

God approaches our minds by receding from them.

We can never fully know Him if we think of Him as an object of capture, to be fenced in by the enclosure of our own ideas.

We know Him better after our minds have let Him go.

The Lord travels in all directions at once.

The Lord arrives from all directions at once.

Wherever we are, we find that He has just departed.

Wherever we go, we discover that He has just arrived before us.

Our rest can be neither in the beginning of this pursuit, nor in the pursuit itself, nor in its apparent end. For the true end, which is Heaven, is an end without end. It is a totally new dimension, in which we come to rest in the secret that He must arrive at the moment of His departure; His arrival is at every moment and His departure is not fixed in time.[2]

The Incarnation

The one Word which God speaks is Himself.[3]

Christ, the Incarnate Word, is the Book of Life in Whom we read God.[4]

Into this world, this demented inn, in which there is absolutely no room for Him at all, Christ has come uninvited. But because He cannot be at home in it, because He is out of place in it, and yet He must be in it, His place is with those others for whom there is no room. His place is with those who do not belong, who are rejected by power because they are regarded as weak, those who are discredited, who are denied the status of persons, tortured, exterminated. With those for whom there is no room, Christ is present in this world.[5]

The Judgement of This World

The advent of God in the world and the judgement of the world take place in each moment of history.[6]

The Passion of God

If on Your Cross Your life and death and mine are one,
Love teaches me to read, in You, the rest of a new history.[7]

There is nothing left now for Him to give. It is now that in a final act He surrenders His life itself. This is "the end of life," not in the sense of a termination, but in the sense of a *culminating gift*, the last free perfect act of love which is at once surrender and acceptance: the surrender of His being into the hands of God, who made it, and the acceptance of the death which in its details and circumstances is perhaps very significantly in continuity with all the acts and incidents of life.... Man's last gift of himself in death is, then, the acceptance of what he has been and the resignation of all final judgement as to the meaning of his life, its worth, its point, its ultimate destiny. It is the final seal his freedom sets upon the love and the trust with which it has striven to live.[8]

Christ alone, on the Cross and in darkness, but already victorious, is our comfort.[9]

A death struggle can also be a struggle for life, a new birth.[10]

Resurrection

O night of admiration, full of choirs,
O night of deepest praise,
And darkness full of triumph:
What secret and intrepid Visitor
Has come to crack our sepulchre?
He softly springs the locks of death
In the foretold encounter.

Why do our steps still hesitate
Upon the threshold of incredible possession,
The sill of the tremendous rest,
Reading the riddle of His unexpected question?

O silence full of execution,
All intuition and desire lie destroyed
When Substance is our Conqueror.
O midnight full of victory,
And silence of the wonderful acclaim,
And darkness full of sweet delight.

O night of admiration, full of choirs,
O night of deepest praise,
And darkness full of sweet delight!
What secret and intrepid Visitor
Has come to raise us from the dead?
He softly springs the locks of time, our sepulchre,
In the foretold encounter.[11]

On Seeing the Lord

And so the disciples at Emmaus—their vocation is our vocation—
came running back to Jerusalem bubbling over with joy and
happiness not because they understood the mysteries of another
world but because they had seen the Lord. That is all we are here
for.[12]

The Christ we seek is within us, in our inmost self, *is* our inmost
self, and yet infinitely transcends ourselves.... The trouble with
the Christian world...[is that] it is enslaved by images and ideas
of Christ that are creations and projections of men.... But Christ
Himself is in us as unknown and unseen. We follow Him, we find
Him...and then He must vanish and we must go along without

Him at our side. Why? Because He is even closer than that. *He is Ourself.*[13]

The Power of Love

Christianity believes so firmly in the power of love, in the Holy Spirit, that it asserts divine love can even overcome death. And it risks death in order to experience the fullness of life.[14]

Life in the Spirit

To be born again is to be born beyond egoism, beyond selfishness, beyond individuality in Christ.

The rebirth of which Christ speaks is not a single event but a continuous dynamic of inner renewal.... True Christianity is growth in the life of the Spirit, a deepening of the new life, a continuous rebirth, in which the exterior and superficial life of the ego-self is discarded like an old snake skin and the mysterious, invisible self of the Spirit becomes more present and active.[15]

Transformation in Christ

It is the Spirit of God that must teach us Who Christ is and form Christ in us and transform us into other Christs. After all, transformation into Christ is not just an individual affair: there is only one Christ, not many. He is not divided. And for me to become Christ is to enter into the Life of the Whole Christ, the Mystical Body made up of the Head and the members, Christ and all who are incorporated in Him by His Spirit.[16]

God does not give His joy to us for ourselves alone, and if we could possess Him for ourselves alone we would not possess Him at all.[17]

To the Ends of the World

Minds, minds, sing like spring
To see the hills that fling their hands into the air:
To see the trees all yield their gladness to the tender winds,
And open wide their treasuries:
Behold the birds, released like angels, from those leafy palaces.
With fire and blue and red-gold splashing in their painted wings,
Each one proclaiming part of the Apocalypse.
They aim their flights at all the four horizons
And fire their arrows of tremendous news.

Beloved Spirit, You are all the prudence and the power
That change our dust and nothing into fields and fruits:
Enfold our lives forever in the compass of Your peaceful hills.[18]

~LOOKING TOWARDS THE END~

It is not inappropriate that the first and last drawings in this anthology should use the circle with all its ancient associations as one of the many enduring symbols of the Living God.

The solidity of the circle still retains a sense of movement, and it serves therefore to remind us not merely of our coming to rest, or of finding our completeness in God, but of the sheer force of creation, redemption, transformation.

The beginning and the end, the end and the beginning: it is a theme that has been explored by poets and preachers, mystics and divines. The mystery of God remains, but at the heart of life and faith there has been for innumerable people down long centuries what Boethius expressed in the early years of the sixth century.

O Father, give the spirit power to climb,
Break through the mists of earth, the weight of the clod,
To see Thee is the end and the beginning,
Thou art the journey, and the journey's end.[1]

To go beyond everything.... and press forward to the End and to the Beginning.[2]

ANTHOLOGY

The End We Live For

See! See!
My Love is darkness!

Only in the Void
Are all ways one:

Only in the night
Are all the lost
Found.

In my ending is my meaning.[3]

⸺⸎⸺

Your life is shaped by the end you live for. You are made in the image of what you desire.[4]

Dying to Life

To find life we must die to life as we know it.[5]

⸺⸎⸺

Yes, death is always something mysterious and in a certain way unacceptable. The very instinct of life itself says that death should not be: and yet it is inevitable. And sometimes the answers of piety are too easy. If, as Christianity believes, God Himself willed in some way to "empty Himself even unto death," then the mystery of it becomes all the greater.[6]

⸺⸎⸺

Perhaps this comes from my thinking about death that has opened out with the last days of Advent—seeing death as built into my life and accepting it in and with life (not trying to push it out of life, keep it away from contaminating a life supposedly complete other than it. Death is flowering in my life as a part and fulfillment of it—its term, its final chord).[7]

Nothing Left but God

Perseverance is not hanging on to some course which we have set our minds to, and refusing to let go…. I am coming to think that God (may He be praised in His great mystery) loves and helps best those who are so beat and have so much nothing when they come to die that it is almost as if they had persevered in nothing but had gradually lost everything, piece by piece, until there was nothing left but God. Hence perseverance is not hanging on but letting go…. But as you say so rightly, it is a question of His hanging on to us.[8]

The Final Beginning

Eschatology is not *finis* and punishment, the winding up of accounts and the closing of books: it is the final beginning, the definitive birth into a new creation. It is not the last gasp of exhausted possibilities but the first taste of all that is beyond conceiving as actual.[9]

— ⊗ —

Eschatology as I understand it is not simply an "end of the world" belief, but, in the light of the New Testament, a belief in the decisive and critical breakthrough in man's destiny. We are on the verge of this breakthrough, in fact it has begun. But we still do not know what form it will take…. Our errors and our luck, our good and evil acts, our honesty and our lies, our love and hate, all our injustices and failures enter into the picture. None of it can be repudiated because it is all there…. But my "eschatology" says that underlying it all, in the deepest depths that we cannot possibly see, lies an ultimate ground in which all contradictions are united and all come out "right."[10]

Union with God

All that matters is union with God.[11]

— ⊗ —

There is something in the depths of our being that hungers for wholeness and finality. Because we are made for eternal life, we are made for an act that gathers all the powers and capacities of our being and offers them simultaneously and forever to God.[12]

I will have more joy in heaven and in the contemplation of God, if you are also there to share it with me; and the more of us there will be to share it the greater will be the joy of all.[13]

To go beyond everything, to leave everything and press forward to the End and to the Beginning, to the ever new Beginning that is without End.[14]

~SOURCES~

The following abbreviations have been used to indicate the most frequent references in the Notes.

AJ   *The Asian Journal of Thomas Merton.* Edited from his Original Notebook by Naomi Burton Stone, Patrick Hart and James Laughlin. Sheldon Press 1974.

AM   Lipsey, Roger, *Angelic Mistakes: The Art of Thomas Merton*, Boston and London: New Seeds 2006.

CGB Merton, Thomas, *Conjectures of a Guilty Bystander*. Sheldon Press 1977.

CP   *The Collected Poems of Thomas Merton.* Sheldon Press 1978.

CPr Merton, Thomas, *Contemplative Prayer*. Darton, Longman and Todd 1973.

CS   *Cistercian Studies*

CWA Merton, Thomas, *Contemplation in a World of Action*. George Allen & Unwin Ltd 1971.

DQ   Merton, Thomas, *Disputed Questions*. Harcourt, Brace & Co 1988.

FV   Merton, Thomas, *Faith and Violence*. Notre Dame Press 1994.

IE   Merton, Thomas, *The Inner Experience*. Edited by William H. Shannon. SPCK 2003.

J i   *The Journals of Thomas Merton.* Volume 1. *Run to the Mountain: The Story of a Vocation.* Edited by Patrick Hart. HarperSanFrancisco 1995.

J ii *The Journals of Thomas Merton.* Volume 2. *Entering the Silence: Becoming a Monk and a Writer.* Edited by Jonathan Montaldo. HarperSanFrancisco 1996.

J iii *The Journals of Thomas Merton.* Volume 3. *A Search for Solitude: Pursuing the Monk's True Life.* Edited by Lawrence S. Cunningham. HarperSanFrancisco 1996.

J iv *The Journals of Thomas Merton.* Volume 4. *Turning Towards the World: The Pivotal Years.* Edited by Victor A. Kramer. HarperSanFrancisco 1996.

J v   *The Journals of Thomas Merton.* Volume 5. *Dancing in the Waters of Life.* Edited by Robert E. Daggy. HarperSanFrancisco 1997.

J vi   *The Journals of Thomas Merton.* Volume 6. *Learning to Love: Exploring Solitude and Freedom.* Edited by Christine M. Bochen. HarperSanFrancisco 1997.

J vii *The Journals of Thomas Merton.* Volume 7. *The Other Side of the Mountain: The End of the Journey.* Edited by Patrick Hart. HarperSanFrancisco 1998.

L i   *The Letters of Thomas Merton* (on Religious Experience and Social Concerns). Volume 1. *The Hidden Ground of Love.* Edited by William H. Shannon. Farrar, Straus, Giroux 1985.

L ii   *The Letters of Thomas Merton* (to New and Old Friends). Volume 2. *The Road to Joy.* Edited by Robert E. Daggy. Farrar, Straus, Giroux 1989.

L iii *The Letters of Thomas Merton* (on Religious Renewal and Spiritual Direction). Volume 3. *The School of Charity.* Edited by Patrick Hart. Farrar, Straus, Giroux 1990.

L iv   *The Letters of Thomas Merton* (to Writers). Volume 4. *The Courage for Truth.* Edited by Christine M. Bochen. Farrar, Straus, Giroux 1993.

L v   *The Letters of Thomas Merton* (in Times of Crisis). Volume 5. *Witness to Freedom.* Edited by William H. Shannon. Farrar, Straus, Giroux 1994.

LE   *The Literary Essays of Thomas Merton.* Edited by Patrick Hart. A New Directions Book 1981.

LL   Merton, Thomas, *Love and Living.* Edited by Naomi Burton Stone and Patrick Hart. A Harvest Book. Harcourt Inc. 1979.

MT   *Thomas Merton / Monk: A Monastic Tribute.* Edited by Patrick Hart. Cistercian Publications 1983.

NM   Merton, Thomas, *The New Man.* Burns & Oates 1964.

NMI   Merton, Thomas, *No Man Is an Island.* Burns & Oates 1993.

NSC   Merton, Thomas, *New Seeds of Contemplation.* Shambhala 2003.

NVA   Merton, Thomas, *The Nonviolent Alternative.* Farrar, Straus, Giroux 1980. The book (apart from the replacement of one article) was originally published under the title *On Peace.*

PPCE Merton, Thomas, *Peace in the Post-Christian Era*. Orbis Books 2004.

RMW Merton, Thomas, Reflection*s on My Work*. Edited by Robert E. Daggy. Collins Fount Paperbacks 1981.

RT Merton, Thomas, *Redeeming the Time*. Burns & Oates 1966.

RU Merton, Thomas, *Raids on the Unspeakable*. Burns & Oates 1993.

SC Merton, Thomas, *Seeds of Contemplation*. Burns & Oates 1960.

SJ Merton, Thomas, *The Sign of Jonas*. Hollis & Carter 1953.

SSM Merton, Thomas, The Seven Storey Mountain. SPCK 1993.

TM Thomas Merton.

TMC Thomas Merton Center, Bellarmine University, Louisville, Kentucky.

TS Merton, Thomas, *Thoughts in Solitude*. Burns & Oates1993.

~NOTES~

FOREWORD

1. Robert Giroux, "Introduction" to *The Seven Storey Mountain*, page xvii. 50th Anniversary Edition (New York: Harcourt Brace, 1998). Trappist monks never took a vow of silence, but observed a rule of silence.

2. Charles Poore, "Books of the Times," *The New York Times* (31 December 1949), 13.

3. Thomas Merton, *Striving Towards Being: The Letters of Thomas Merton and Czeslaw Milosz*, p. 175. Ed. Robert Faggen (New York: Farrar, Straus and Giroux, 1997).

4. In a similar vein the Hindu scholar Amiya Chakravarty wrote to him: "The absolute rootedness of your faith makes you free to understand other faiths." Amiya Chakravarty to TM (29 March 1967).

5. Cornelia Jessey, "Griffin and Friendships." In *Way of St Francis* XXXVII.7 (September 1981), 59 and 61.

6. L iv 217.

7. Thomas Merton, *New Seeds of Contemplation* (New York: New Directions 1961), 297.

PREFACE

1. "First and Last Thoughts: An Author's Preface." *A Thomas Merton Reader*. Ed. Thomas P. McDonnell (New York: Image Books, Doubleday, 1996), 16.

2. Ibid.

3. Ibid.

4. Merton Annual 9 (1996). (*"The Great Honesty": Remembering Thomas Merton*). Interview by George Kilcross with Abbot Timothy Kelly.

5. Merton Annual 14 (2001). (*A Journey into Wholeness*). Interview by Christine Bochen and Victor Kramer with Sister Myriam Dardenne at Redwoods Monastery.

6. AM.

7. This technique is explored by John Begley, James Grubola, and John Whitesell in the article "Thomas Merton, Printmaker: Reconstructing His Technique." AM 167–173.

8. Elena Malits, CSC, Review of *The Collected Poems of Thomas Merton*. *Notre Dame English Journal* 14 (October 1978).

9. L v 10. TM to Victor Hammer (3 November 1964).

10. Letter. TM to Sister Gabriel Mary (28 April 1965). TMC Collection.

11. J v 139 (29 August 1964).

12. Merton, Thomas, "Signatures: Notes on the Author's Drawings." AM 60–61. Article to accompany the exhibition of Merton's abstract drawings at Catherine Spalding College in Louisville, November 1964.

13. Ibid.

14. L iv 217. TM to Margaret Randall and Sergio Mondragon (9 October 1963).
15. AM 61.
16. Ibid.

PART ONE
1. J v 160 (31 October 1964).
2. LE 319 (Jorge Carrera Andrade).
3. NMI 209.
4. NMI xi.
5. CPr 84.
6. CGB 313.
7. NSC 49.

Encountering God
1. CP 186. *Freedom as Experience*, from *Figures for an Apocalypse* (1947).
2. NSC 12.
3. NSC 41.
4. SC 13.
5. NSC 12.
6. CWA 344.
7. L i 565. TM to Daisetz T. Suzuki (11 April 1959).
8. CP 176. *The Transformation: For the Sacred Heart*, from *Figures for an Apocalypse* (1947).
9. NMI 209.
10. L i 158. TM to Dom Francis Decroix in response to the request from Pope Paul VI that there might be a message from contemplatives to the world (21 August 1967).
11. CPr 111.
12. CWA 344.
13. SJ 279 (10 March 1950).
14. J ii 475 (June 1952).

Exploring the Depths
1. Catherine of Siena, *Dialogue*, Chapter 167.
2. SC 211.
3. SC 85.
4. NSC 211.
5. NSC 138.
6. DQ 212.
7. LL 20.
8. TM.
9. SC 85–86.
10. AJ 296. Circular Letter to Friends (September 1968).
11. J iii 67 (19 August 1956).
12. LL 40–41.

13. J ii 187 (19 March 1948).
14. LE 319 (Jorge Carrera Andrade).
15. L i 157. TM to Dom Francis Decroix (21 August 1967).
16. NSC 134.
17. CGB 161.
18. NMI 227.
19. J ii 54 (Palm Sunday, 30 March 1947).

Discerning the Truth

1. CWA 344.
2. J ii 476 (June 1951).
3. RMW 101. Preface to the Japanese edition of SC (1965).
4. L v 254. TM to Mr. Wainwright (10 July 1965).
5. CGB 181.
6. NSC 158–159.
7. J ii 476 (June 1951).
8. NMI xi.
9. CPr 84.
10. J i 339 (9 April 1941).

Finding My True Self

1. CP 199. *Hymn for the Feast of Duns Scotus*, from *Tears of the Blind Lions* (1949).
2. CPr 84.
3. CPr 84.
4. J ii 155 (4 January 1948).
5. TS 31.
6. NSC 286–287.
7. NMI xv–xvi.
8. J ii 199 (11 April 1948).
9. SJ 272 (22 February 1950).
10. NMI 112.
11. NSC 49.
12. NMI xvi.
13. Merton, Thomas, *In Silence*, from *In the Dark Before Dawn* (New York: New Directions Book, 2005), 90–91.
14. J v 223 (3 April 1965).
15. NSC 38.
16. NM 26.

Part Two

1. LL 4.
2. MA 4 (1992) 203. A.M. Allchin, *The Worship of the Whole Creation: Merton and the Eastern Fathers*.
3. RMW 110, From the preface to the Korean edition of *Life and Holiness* (1965).

4. LL 198.
5. RMW 110 (*op. cit.*)
6. Wilkes, Paul, Editor, *Merton by Those Who Knew Him Best* (New York: Harper & Row, 1984), 123. (John Eudes Bamberger).
7. Merton, Thomas, cited by Daphne V. Steere in the foreword to *The Climate of Monastic Prayer*. Cistercian Studies: Number One (Shannon, Ireland, 1969).
8. J i 356 (12 April 1941).
9. CS v (1970) 3 222. Merton, Thomas, *A Life Free from Care*. Article transcribed from a tape recording for a conference Merton gave to the novitiate on 20 August 1965 before going to the hermitage.
10. J iii 132 (2 November 1957).
11. L i 52. TM to Abdul Aziz (4 April 1962).
12. *What Ought I to Do?* (1959); *The Wisdom of the Desert* (1960).
13. IE 103.
14. NM 2–3.
15. LL 140.
16. LL 27.
17. J ii 463 (29 November 1951).
18. NSC 63.
19. DQ 122.
20. DQ 99.

Living the Gospel
1. J v 160 (31 October 1964).
2. NMI 204.
3. Thomas Merton, prologue to *The Silent Life*, (London: Sheldon Press), vii.
4. LL 198.
5. LL 196.
6. RMW 110. From the preface to the Korean edition of *Life and Holiness* (1965).
7. Ibid.
8. L iii 93. TM to Dom Jean Leclercq (3 December 1955).
9. J ii 11 (Good Friday, 3 April 1942).
10. TS 81.
11. L ii 22. TM to Mark van Doren (30 March 1948).
12. J v 160 (31 October 1964).

The Meaning of Faith
1. SSM 419.
2. CGB 18.
3. L iv 225. TM to Ludovico Silva (10 April 1965).
4. FV 279.
5. Thomas Merton, cited by Douglas V. Steere in the foreword to *The Climate of Monastic Prayer*. Cistercian Series: Number One (Shannon, Ireland, 1969).
6. J ii 199 (11 April 1948).

7. J ii 8 (1 February 1942).
8. AJ 306 (Appendix III).
9. FV 213.
10. J ii 76 (23 May 1947).
11. SSM 419.
12. J i 356 (12 April 1941).

Armor for the Fight
1. Words from the Office Hymn at Terce, St Mary's Abbey, West Malling, Kent, United Kingdom.
2. J v 287 (28 August 1965).
3. J iii 135 (12 November 1957).
4. J ii 350 (8 August 1949).
5. NMI 133–134.
6. NMI 25.
7. L iv 269. TM to Lawrence Ferlinghetti (2 August 1961).
8. CS v (1970) 3 222. Merton, Thomas, *A Life Free from Care*. Article transcribed from a tape recording of a conference Merton gave to the novitiate on 20 August 1965 before going to the hermitage.
9. Ron Seitz, *Song for Nobody: A Memory Vision of Thomas Merton* (Triumph Books, Ligouri, Missouri 1993), 172–173.
10. J i 304 (4 February 1941).
11. CPr 98.
12. L i 159. TM to Dom Francis Decroix (22 August 1967).
13. J vii 135 (29 June 1968).
14. J v 287 (28 August 1965).
15. J vi 234 (13 May 1967).
16. CGB 221.
17. L ii 62. TM to Agnes Gertrude Stonehewer Merton, "Aunt Kit," (27 May 1964).
18. CGB 118.

Siren Voices
1. SJ 236 (16 November 1949).
2. FV 154.
3. RMW 96 (Preface to the Japanese edition of SC, 1959).
4. SJ 236 (16 November 1949).
5. RMW 109 (Preface to the Korean edition of *Life and Holiness*, 1965).
6. J iii 132 (2 November 1957).
7. L iv 75. TM to Czeslaw Milosz (5 June 1961).
8. LL 42.
9. J ii 65 (23 April 1947).
10. J ii 80–81 (31 May 1947).
11. J i 449 (4 November 1941).
12. L v 329. TM to Katharine Champney (10 November 1966).

13. SJ 235 (7 October 1949).
14. CP 452 (from *Cables to the Ace*, 1968).
15. SJ 266 (5 February 1950).

The Desert

1. CP 319. *Macarius the Younger*, from *Emblems of a Season of Fury* (1963).
2. J ii 463 (29 November 1951).
3. CP 319. *Macarius the Younger*, from *Emblems of a Season of Fury* (1965).
4. SJ 49 (13 June 1947).
5. L iii 48. TM to Dom Gabriel Sortais (4 November 1952).
6. CP 191. *The Landfall*, from *Figures for an Apocalypse* (1947).
7. IE 103.
8. J ii 233 (13 September 1948).
9. J vi 309 (18 June 1966).
10. L iv 57–58. TM to Czeslaw Milosz (28 February 1959).
11. CP 125. *St John Baptist*, from *A Man in the Divided Sea* (1946).
12. NSC 55.
13. MT 83–84. David Steindl-Rast, *Man of Prayer*, in which Steindl-Rast draws extensively upon conversations with TM at the Community of Our Lady of the Redwoods Abbey, Whitehorn, California, October 1968.
14. J ii 463 (29 November 1951).
15. CP 24 (*Sacred Heart 2*, from *Early Poems*, 1940–42).

The Paradox of Hope

1. CP 53. *An Argument: Of the Passion of Christ*, from *Thirty Poems* (1944).
2. NM 2–3.
3. RU 5.
4. Ron Seitz, 172.
5. CP 265. *The Tower of Babel*, from *The Strange Islands* (1957).
6. NMI 162.
7. J iii 57–58 (29 July 1956).
8. L i 297. TM to James Forest (21 February 1966).
9. NM 2–3.
10. LL 22.
11. LL 140.
12. RT 93.

The Priority of Love

1. Thomas à Kempis, *The Imitation of Christ*, book 3, chapter 5.
2. LL 27.
3. LL 27.
4. J ii 64 (20 April 1947).
5. NSC 63.

6. LL 27.
7. DQ 122.
8. DQ 123.
9. NMI 4.
10. DQ 99.
11. DQ 100.
12. LL 17.
13. LL 35–36.
14. J ii 174 (29 February 1948).
15. J ii 236 (10 October 1948).

PART THREE
1. SSM 111.
2. Paul Wilkes, *Merton by Those Who Knew Him Best* (New York: Harper & Row 1984), 105.
3. Cornelia Jessey, cited by Dr. Paul M. Pearson in the foreword to this anthology.
4. NSC 227.
5. MT 81 (David Steindl-Rast, *op. cit.*).
6. CS xiii (1978) 3 192. Thomas Merton, *Towards a Theology of Prayer*. Edited transcript of a taped talk given by TM to the Jesuit Scholasticate at St Mary's College, Darjeeling, India, on 25 November 1968.
7. MT 81 (David Steindl-Rast).
8. L i 371. TM to Etta Gullick (9 June 1965) (2 January 1966).
9. L i 63–64. TM to Abdul Aziz.
10. MT 80 (David Steindl-Rast).
11. MT 79 (David Steindl-Rast).
12. NSC 219.
13. J ii 300 (6 April 1949).
14. LL 42.
15. SC 25.
16. L i 73. TM to Daniel J. Berrigan (10 March 1962).
17. CPr 25.
18. SJ 28 (11 March 1947).
19. RMW 51–52. Preface to the Argentine edition of *The Complete Works of TM* (1958).
20. Merton, Thomas, *The Waters of Siloe* (New York: Doubleday Image Books, 1962), 262–263.
21. SJ 275 (3 March 1950).

Learning to Pray
1. CPr 48.
2. L i 159. TM to Dom Francis Decroix (22 August 1967).
3. L iii 297. TM to Dame B (30 January 1966).
4. NSC 227.

5. CS xiii (1978) 3 192. Thomas Merton, *Toward a Theology of Prayer*. Edited transcript of a taped talk given by TM to the Jesuit Scholasticate at St Mary's College, Darjeeling, India, on 25 November 1968.
6. J iii 46 (17 July 1956).
7. MT 87 (David Steindl-Rast, *op. cit.*).
8. MT 81 (David Steindl-Rast, *op. cit.*).
9. Ibid.
10. NSC 219.
11. CPr 48.
12. J ii 100 (17 August 1947).
13. NMI 36.
14. CPr 143.
15. CPr 139.

The Experience of Prayer

1. Sister Wendy Beckett, *The Gaze of Love* (Marshall Pickering, 1993), 28.
2. CP 109. *After the Night Office—Gethsemani Abbey*, from *A Man in the Divided Sea* (1946).
3. TS 91.
4. TS 91.
5. L i 63–64. TM to Abdul Aziz (2 January 1966).
6. CPr 86.
7. MT 80 (David Steindl-Rast, *op. cit.*).
8. MT 79 (David Steindl-Rast, *op. cit.*).
9. NSC 247.
10. Thomas Merton, *Day of a Stranger* (Salt Lake City: Gibbs M. Smith, 1981), 41.
11. J v 347 (Some Personal Notes. End of 1965).
12. L ii 196. TM to Sister Thérèse Lentfoehr (3 October 1949).
13. NSC 219.
14. L i 371. TM to Etta Gullick (9 June 1965).
15. L i 73. TM to Daniel J. Berrigan (10 March 1962).
16. NSC 224.
17. L i 376. TM to Etta Gullick (1 August 1966).
18. CPr 40.
19. MT 88 (David Steindl-Rast, *op. cit.*).
20. CPr 13.
21. TS 36.
22. J iii 359 (17 December 1959).

Solitude and Silence

1. CP 340–341. *Song: If You Seek ...* from *Emblems of a Season of Fury* (1963).
2. SC 31.
3. DQ 196.
4. NSC 82–83.

5. DQ 178.
6. MT 76 (Sister Thérèse Lentfoehr, *The Solitary*).
7. LL 22.
8. DQ 197.
9. J v 335 (Some Personal Notes. End of 1965).
10. SC 31.
11. NSC 83–84.
12. LL 42.
13. NSC 134.
14. RMW 127 (Preface to Japanese edition of TS, 1966).
15. RMW 124 (Preface to Japanese edition of TS, 1966).
16. SC 25.
17. CGB 18.
18. RU 16.
19. LL 17.
20. TS 93.

The Contemplative Vocation
1. CP 201. *The Quickening of St John the Baptist*, from *The Tears of the Blind Lion* (1949).
2. J vii 262 (7 November 1968).
3. NSC 3.
4. LE 340. *Poetry and Contemplation: A Reappraisal.*
5. From Notes identified by Sister Thérèse Lentfoehr and taken at the retreat conducted by TM for the Superiors of contemplative nuns at Gethsemani in December 1967.
6. CGB 7.
7. FV 217.
8. SJ 28 (11 March 1947).
9. NSC 273.
10. L ii 319. TM to Joseph Tjo Tchel-oung (28 April 1961).
11. LE 339 (*Poetry and Contemplation: A Reappraisal*).
12. J vii 262 (7 November 1968).
13. CWA 363.
14. IE 66.
15. IE 147.
16. IE 66.
17. NSC 79.
18. Thomas Merton, *The Waters of Siloe* (New York: Doubleday Image Books, 1962), 262–263.
19. NSC 274.
20. SJ 275 (3 March 1950).
21. NMI 61.
22. RMW 51–52. Preface to Argentine edition of *The Complete Works of TM* (1958).

PART FOUR

1. Thomas Merton, *The Climate of Monastic Prayer*, 35.
2. CGB 153.
3. Thomas Merton, "Is the World a Problem?" *Commonweal* 84(3) (June 1968).
4. J iii 200 (5 May 1958).
5. Merton, Thomas, "Is the World a Problem?" (*op. cit.*).
6. Merton, Thomas, *A Life Free from Care* (*op. cit.*).
7. J iv 312 (11 April 1963).
8. J v 227 (15 April 1965).
9. CGB 313.
10. CGB 204.
11. L v 7. TM to Victor Hammer (May 1962).
12. DQ 147.
13. L v 249. TM to William Robert Miller (June 1962).
14. AJ 317 (Appendix IV).
15. CGB 317–318.
16. NVA 67.
17. Thomas Merton, *Thoughts on the East* (Burns & Oates 1996), 61.
18. J vii 47 (26 January 1968).
19. NVA 105–106.
20. DQ 124.
21. Thomas Merton, *The New Man* (Mentor Omega, 1963), 46.
22. Prologue to NMI xx.

Embracing the World

1. J iii 200 (5 May 1958)
2. CWA 164–165.
3. Thomas Merton, "Is the World a Problem?"
4. LL 120.
5. Thomas Merton, "Is the World a Problem?" (*op. cit.*).
6. CGB 44.
7. FV 138.
8. J v 171 (30 November 1964).
9. L i 186. TM to Sister M. Emmanuel (16 January 1962).
10. CGB 216.
11. FV 256.
12. LL 153.
13. RT 67.
14. L i 55. TM to Abdul Aziz (2 June 1963).
15. NSC 68.
16. J iii 200 (5 May 1958).

Delighting in the Whole Creation

1. CP 188. *The Sowing of Meanings*, from *Figures for an Apocalypse* (1947).

2. Thomas Merton, *A Life Free from Care*, (*op. cit.*).
3. NMI 28.
4. Thomas Merton, *Bread in the Wilderness* (London: Hollis & Carter, 1954), 54.
5. CGB 287.
6. Thomas Merton, *A Life Free from Care*. (*op. cit.*).
7. CGB 174.
8. J ii 423 (21 March 1950).
9. Thomas Merton, *Commentary on the Meditations of Guigo, the Carthusian*. TMC. The Merton Tapes, Tape 7: *Life and Truth*).
10. J v 212 (2 March 1965).
11. L v 71. TM to Rachel Carson (12 January 1963).
12. J iv 312 (13 April 1963).
13. Thomas Merton, *The Secular Journal of Thomas Merton* (London: Sheldon Press 1977), 13.
14. CP 184 (*Natural History* from *Figures for an Apocalypse*, 1947).
15. J v 227 (15 April 1965).
16. J iv 274 (11 December 1962).
17. J iv 312 (11 April 1963).
18. CGB 136.
19. CP 188–189 (*The Sowing of Meanings* from *Figures for an Apocalypse*, 1947).

The Present Moment
1. CGB 204.
2. RMW 59. Preface to the French edition of *Monastic Peace* (1960).
3. L v 337. TM to Water A. Weisskopf (4 April 1968).
4. L v 180. TM to Sister Anita Wasserman OCD (21 May 1953).
5. CGB 312–313.
6. J ii 460 (13 June 1951).
7. CGB 204.
8. RT 93.
9. RU 2–3.
10. CGB 216.
11. L i 20. TM to Catherine de Hueck Doherty (12 November 1962).
12. SJ 104 (24 June 1948).
13. SJ 353 (Epilogue: *Fire Watch*, 4 July 1952).

The Prevailing Scene
1. L v 249. TM to William Robert Miller (June 1962).
2. CGB 63–64.
3. NVA 221 (from *Christian Action in World Crisis*).
4. L v 7. TM to Victor Hammer (May 1962).
5. FV 153.
6. FV 174.
7. DQ 147.

8. RU 49–50.
9. CP 372. *A Letter to Pablo Antonio Cuadra Concerning Giants*, from *Emblems of a Season of Fury* (1963).
10. Thomas Merton, *Classic Chinese Thought*, Jubilee (January 1961).
11. CP 380. *A Letter to Pablo Antonio Cuadra Concerning Giants* (*op. cit.*).
12. AJ 317 (Appendix IV).
13. J iii 150 (29 December 1957).
14. J v 44 (11 December 1963).
15. CGB 5 (Preface).
16. L v 249. TM to William Robert Miller (June 1962).
17. PPCE 72.
18. CGB 114.
19. LL 17.
20. CGB 317–318.
21. L iv 237. TM to Cinto Vitier (1 August 1963).
22. L v 276. TM to Louis Massignon (18 March 1960).
23. J ii 43 (10 March 1947).

Violence and Nonviolence

1. CP 185. *A Christmas Card*, from *Figures for an Apocalypse* (1947).
2. DQ 65.
3. PPCE 7.
4. NVA 67.
5. Thomas Merton, *Thoughts on the East*, 61. Burns & Oates 1996.
6. CP 131 (*La Salette*, from *A Man in the Divided Sea*, 1946).
7. CGB 39.
8. FV 167.
9. J vii 47 (26 January 1968).
10. J ii 451 (3 March 1951).
11. Thomas Merton, *Christian Ethics and Nuclear War* (The Catholic Worker, 28 March 1962).
12. NSC 125.
13. LE 28 (*A Footnote from Ulysses: Peace and Revolution*).
14. FV 20.
15. NVA 105–106.
16. DQ 65.

On Being Human

1. RU 6.
2. CWA 100.
3. RU 6.
4. Thomas Merton, "Is the World a Problem?" (*op. cit.*).
5. FV 142–143.
6. TMR 16 (*First and Last Thoughts: An Author's Preface*).

7. L v 255. TM to Robert Menchin (15 January 1966).
8. CGB 170.
9. CGB 222.
10. DQ 124.
11. NMI 22.
12. NSC 63.
13. NMI 56.
14. CP 389. *A Letter to Pablo Antonio Cuadra Concerning Giants* (*op. cit.*).
15. J iii 45 (17 July 1956).

A Christian Humanism
1. NSC 301.
2. CP 384. *A Letter to Pablo Antonion Cuadra Concerning Giants.* (*op. cit.*).
3. CP 390. *A Letter to Pablo Antonio Cuadra Concerning Giants* (*op. cit.*).
4. CGB 154.
5. J v 279 (13 August 1965).
6. NSC 301.
7. RT 40.
8. Thomas Merton, *On Zen* (Sheldon Press 1976), 108.
9. Thomas Merton, *The New Man*, 46. Mentor Omega 1963.
10. RT 65.
11. J i 399 (3 September 1941).
12. CGB 141.
13. RU 52.
14. CP 382–383. *A Letter to Pablo Antonio Cuadra Concerning Giants* (*op. cit.*).
15. CP 384–385. *A Letter to Pablo Antonio Cuadra Concerning Giants* (*op. cit.*).
16. CGB 154.
17. NMI Prologue, xx–xxi.

PART FIVE
1. PPCE 72.
2. RMW 51. Preface to the Argentine edition of *The Complete Works of Thomas Merton* (1958).
3. Thomas Merton, *On Peace*, 122.
4. L v 249. TM to William Robert Miller (June 1962).
5. FV 209.
6. RT 102.
7. RT 69.
8. J iv 9 (6 June 1960).
9. J iii 211 (3 August 1958).
10. J iv 9 (6 June 1960).
11. CGB 266.
12. L i 58. TM to Abdul Aziz (28 June 1964).
13. J vi 358–359. Some Personal Notes (January–March 1966).

14. CGB 319.
15. CP 384–385 *A Letter to Pablo Antonio Cuadra Concerning Giants.*
16. L i 126. TM to Dona Luisa Coomaraswamy (13 January 1961).
17. AJ 308 (Appendix III).

The Church Looking Beyond Itself

1. RMW 51. Preface to the Argentine edition of *The Complete Works of Thomas Merton* (1958).
2. NVA 13–14.
3. PPCE 72.
4. J iv 138 (4 July 1961).
5. L v 249. TM to William Robert Miller (June 1962).
6. Thomas Merton, *On Peace*, 122.
7. L i 186. TM to Sister M. Emmanuel (16 January 1962).
8. RMW 50–51. Preface to the Argentine edition of *The Complete Works of Thomas Merton* (1958).
9. FV 209.
10. RT 102.
11. FV 259.
12. Related by Sister Mary Luke Tobin from a conversation with TM after his final address at Bangkok, 10 December 1968. Sister Mary Luke Tobin, *Merton: A Pictorial Biography*, 99.

On Building the Kingdom of God

1. J iii 211 (3 August 1958).
2. DQ 127.
3. DQ 142.
4. CGB 88.
5. DQ 128.
6. RT 69.
7. NVA 222.
8. J iv 9 (6 June 1960).
9. Thomas Merton, "Is the World a Problem?" (*op. cit.*).
10. J iii 211 (3 August 1958).
11. FV 16.
12. CP 263 (*The Tower of Babel*, from *The Strange Islands*, 1957).

A Wider Ecumenism

1. AJ 308 (Appendix III).
2. Thomas Merton, *Mystics and Zen Masters*, x. Farrar, Straus and Giroux, 1999.
3. CGB 266.
4. RU 28.
5. CGB 141.
6. J vi 358–359 (Some Personal Notes. January–March 1966).
7. L i 58. TM to Abdul Aziz (28 June 1964).

8. CP 384–385 (*A Letter to Pablo Antonio Cuadra Concerning Giants, op. cit.*).
9. CGB 319.
10. CP 384–385 (*A Letter to Pablo Antonio Cuadra Concerning Giants, op. cit.*).
11. L i 126. TM to Dona Luisa Coomaraswamy (13 January 1961).
12. AJ 308 (Appendix III).

PART SIX
1. J vii 278 (16 November 1968).
2. NSC 301.
3. LL 153.
4. Merton, Thomas, *Bread in the Wilderness* (London: Hollis & Carter 1954), 86.
5. RMW 146–147, Preface to the Japanese edition of *The New Man* (1967).
6. NSC 166.
7. CP 105. *The Biography*, from *A Man in the Divided Sea* (1946).
8. NVA 219.
9. NM 6.
10. L v 337–338. TM to Water A. Weisskopf (4 April 1968).
11. J iv 101 (22 March 1961).

On Being in Christ
1. CP 370–371. *Hagia Sophia*, from *Emblems of a Season of Fury* (1963).
2. Thomas Merton, *Bread in the Wilderness* (London: Hollis & Carter 1954), 86.
3. RMW 111–112. Preface to Korean edition of *Life and Holiness* (1965).
4. From TM's statement at the opening of the TM Collection at Bellarmine College Library, November 1963; Michael Mott, *The Seven Mountains of Thomas Merton* (Houghton Mifflin Company, 1984), 392.
5. L i 359. TM to Etta Gullick (29 April 1963).
6. CP 380. *A Letter to Pablo Antonio Cuadra Concerning Giants* (*op. cit.*).
7. RT 122.
8. Thomas Merton, *Bread in the Wilderness* (London: Hollis & Carter, 1954), 86.
9. NSC 67.
10. NSC 166.
11. AJ 334 (Appendix VII).
12. J i 223 (26 May 1940).
13. L v 85. TM to Evora Arca de Sardinia (5 September 1964).
14. NSC 37.

The Mysteries of Faith
1. TS 62.
2. NMI 210–211.
3. RMW 126. Preface to Japanese edition of TS (1966).
4. TS 62.
5. RU 51–52.
6. L iii 108. TM to Jaime Andrade (3 March 1958).
7. CP 105. *The Biography*, from *A Man in the Divided Sea* (1946).

8. LL 102–103.
9. CGB 162.
10. NVA 219.
11. CP 112–113. *The Dark Encounter*, from *A Man in the Divided Sea* (1946).
12. Thomas Merton, *A Life Free from Care* (*op. cit.*).
13. L i 564. TM to Daisetz T. Suzuki (11 April 1959).
14. NM 9.
15. RMW 146–147. Preface to Japanese edition of *The New Man* (1967).
16. NSC 159–160.
17. NSC 274.
18. CP 119–121. *A Whitsun Canticle*, from *A Man in the Divided Sea* (1946).

Looking Towards the End

1. Boethius (c. 480–c. 524). Translated by Helen Waddell.
2. J iv 101 (22 March 1961).
3. CP 635. "Appendix I: Sensation Time at the Home," *The Night of Destiny* (1968).
4. TS 55.
5. NM 6.
6. L iv 211. TM to Victoria Ocampo (14 July 1968).
7. J v 327 (25 December 1965).
8. L i 137. TM to Dorothy Day (4 February 1960).
9. RU 54.
10. L v 337–338. TM to Water A. Weisskopf (4 April 1968).
11. J ii 81 (31 May 1947).
12. NMI 124.
13. NSC 67–68.
14. J iv 101 (22 March 1961).

ABOUT THE AUTHOR

John Moses is an Anglican priest who continues to be fascinated by Thomas Merton—the challenge of his discipleship, the contradictions he presents, and the contributions he continues to make to issues of contemporary concern. His earlier books include studies of John Donne (*One Equall Light*), prayer (*The Language of Love*), and Thomas Merton (*Divine Discontent: The Prophetic Voice of Thomas Merton*). He is Dean Emeritus of St. Paul's Cathedral, London, UK.